THE ENTERPRISE OF WAR

TimeFrame

MAGAZIN ROYAL DE

appellé vulgairement

ARMES A PARIS. de la Bastille

TIME® **LIFE** BOOKS

This volume is one in a series that tells the story
of humankind. Other books in the series include:

THE ENTERPRISE OF WAR

TimeFrame

BY THE EDITORS OF TIME-LIFE BOOKS

TIME-LIFE BOOKS, ALEXANDRIA, VIRGINIA

Time-Life Books is a division of Time
Life Inc., a wholly owned subsidiary of
THE TIME INC. BOOK COMPANY

TIME-LIFE BOOKS

Managing Editor: Thomas H. Flaherty
Director of Editorial Resources:
Elise D. Ritter-Clough
Director of Photography and Research:
John Conrad Weiser
Editorial Board: Dale M. Brown, Roberta
Conlan, Laura Foreman, Lee Hassig, Jim
Hicks, Blaine Marshall, Rita Thievon
Mullin, Henry Woodhead

PUBLISHER: Joseph J. Ward

Associate Publisher: Ann M. Mirabito
Editorial Director: Russell B. Adams
Marketing Director: Anne Everhart
Director of Design: Louis Klein
Production Manager: Prudence G. Harris
Supervisor of Quality Control:
James King

EUROPEAN EDITOR: Ellen Phillips
Design Director: Ed Skyner
Director of Editorial Resources:
Samantha Hill
Chief Sub-Editor: Ilse Gray

Correspondents: Elisabeth Kraemer-Singh
(Bonn); Maria Vincenza Aloisi (Paris);
Ann Natanson (Rome). Valuable assis-
tance was also provided by: Louise D.
Forstall (Alexandria, Virginia); Elizabeth
Brown (New York); Josephine du Brusle
(Paris); Traudl Lessing (Vienna).

TIME FRAME
(published in Britain as
TIME-LIFE HISTORY OF THE WORLD)

SERIES EDITOR: Charles Boyle

Editorial Staff for *The Enterprise of War*
Editor: Christopher Farman
Designer: Rachel Gibson
Researchers: Caroline Smith (principal),
Kathy Lockley
Sub-Editors: Tim Cooke, Luci Collings
Editorial Assistant: Molly Sutherland

Picture Department
Picture Administrator: Amanda Hindley
Picture Coordinator: Elizabeth Turner

Editorial Production
Production Assistant: Emma Veys
Editorial Department: Theresa John,
Debra Lelliott

U.S. EDITION

Assistant Editor: Barbara Fairchild
Quarmby
Senior Copy Coordinator: Ann Lee Bruen
Picture Coordinator: David Beard

Editorial Operations
Production: Celia Beattie
Library: Louise D. Forstall
Computer Composition: Deborah G. Tait
(Manager), Monika D. Thayer, Janet
Barnes Syring, Lillian Daniels

Special Contributors: Douglas Botting, Neil
Fairbairn, Michael Kerrigan, Alan Lothian,
Charles Messenger (text); David E. Manley
(index).

CONSULTANTS

General and Early Modern:
GEOFFREY PARKER, Professor of History,
University of Illinois, Urbana-Champaign, Il-
linois

Classical:
PHILIP SABIN, Lecturer in the Department
of War Studies, King's College, University of
London

Medieval:
MICHAEL PRESTWICH, Professor of History, University of Durham, Durham, England

Modern:
BRIAN BOND, Professor of Military History,
King's College, University of London

Library of Congress Cataloging in
Publication Data

The Enterprise of war / by the editors of
Time-Life Books.
      p.   cm. — (Time frame)
   Includes bibliographical references and
index.
   ISBN 0-8094-6495-0 (trade)
   ISBN 0-8094-6496-9 (lib. bdg.)
   1. Military art and science—History.
   2. Military history.
I. Time-Life Books. II. Series.
U27.E57 1991
355'.009—dc20   91-3339
                                        CIP

CONTENTS

THE FIRST ARMIES

Arcing swiftly through the air, a tail of rope uncoiling behind it, the iron grappling hook caught in the building's fire-licked timber frame, slipped a few inches, then held fast. A sharp tug showed that it was firmly fixed, and at their centurion's nodded command, the legionaries below lay back against the rope and hauled away, grunting with the effort. Suddenly the line went slack, and the troops scattered as an avalanche of shattered masonry and burning wood crashed down into the street. A large section of wall had been torn away, and the women and children sheltering in the building's top three floors were now plainly visible to the attackers. Eyes streaming from the dust and smoke, they crowded to the edge of their tottering apartments to make their last despairing pleas for compassion—and to gaze in fear and bewilderment on the faces of the soldiers who had no compassion.

After more than six centuries, the proud city of Carthage was in its final death throes. Its ordeal had begun three years earlier in 149 BC, when the Romans had placed it under siege. At that stage, the city had seemed impregnable. Built on a promontory projecting into the Bay of Tunis, it was protected to the east by the Mediterranean Sea and to the north, south, and west by walls almost thirty feet thick and forty feet high. Cut off from supplies by the Roman blockade, however, the city's defenders became desperate with hunger, and many died or gave themselves up. The final blow fell in the spring of 146 BC with the capture by the Romans of part of the ramparts. Soon the center of the city was in their hands, and from there, they began a grim, step-by-step advance up the Byrsa hill toward the inner citadel.

The streets in this area were flanked by six-story houses from which the Carthaginians poured down a shower of missiles. The Romans replied by destroying each house in turn, then setting it on fire, demolishing the ruins. In the wake of the demolition squads, other troops packed down the debris, the bodies of the dead and dying flung in haphazardly alongside the rubble and smoldering timber. After six days and nights of continuous and bitter fighting, the Romans reached the citadel. On the seventh day, it surrendered, and 50,000 men, women, and children—starving and demoralized—came forth to be sold into slavery. Hasdrubal, the Carthaginian commander, soon followed, but his wife preferred to throw herself and her two children into the burning temple where some of the defenders had decided to fight to the last. For ten more days, the fires of Carthage raged. Finally, everything that was still standing was leveled, the site was plowed, and the furrows were sown with salt—the sign that it was to remain a wasteland forever. Thus ended another bleak episode in the enterprise of war.

Conflict was not always the way of humanity. The small bands of nomadic hunter-gatherers who roamed the earth during the first 90,000 years of human existence

Emboldening his adherents and inspiring fear and trembling in their enemies, the angry countenance of this carved wooden image of a war god presides over a temple in Hawaii in the nineteenth century. From the time the islands of Hawaii were first settled by Polynesian migrants around AD 400, land disputes between rival tribes frequently erupted into warfare. Religious rituals—including human sacrifice, the interpretation of omens, and the carrying of images of gods into battle—bolstered the rule of powerful chiefs and cemented the loyalty of their subjects. As in other belligerent societies—such as Rome, whose war god Mars was originally an agricultural deity—a primary function of religion was to justify war and reinforce martial values.

The Roman standard-bearer and infantryman shown in a detail from a relief *(above)* represent the fundamental and most enduring component of all armies until the fall of the Roman Empire—the common foot soldier, hardened by rigorous training and equipped with sling, sword, or spear. The drawing on the right illustrates the basic pattern of a Roman military sandal: The loops, cut from a single piece of leather, were tied with laces around the ankle and foot; the sole, made of several layers of leather stuck together, was shod with iron studs. Sufficient for their purpose, it was on footwear such as this that empires were conquered.

appear to have been predominantly peaceful and cooperative, such violence as did occur being sporadic and unorganized. A glimpse of what that vanished world might have been like was afforded the Norwegian explorer Fridtjof Nansen, who made an epic journey across the mighty Greenland icecap in 1888. The Inuit peoples whom Nansen encountered still lived in much the same way as their early forebears, scattered in small, self-sufficient groups and taking from the land only what they needed for their immediate purposes. He noted:

> *Fighting and brutalities of that sort . . . are unknown among them, and murder is very rare. They hold it atrocious to kill a fellow creature; therefore, war is in their eyes incomprehensible and repulsive, a thing for which their language has no word; and soldiers and officers, brought up in the trade of killing, they regard as mere butchers.*

How and when humans first resorted to serious conflict are questions that have yet to be finally answered. But the archaeological evidence—burial sites, cave paintings, fortifications, artifacts—suggests that it was only some 10,000 years ago that large-scale combat became an inseparable part of human existence. What appears to have sparked the change in behavior was the rise of settled agricultural communities. In addition to attracting the envy of groups that continued to follow the nomadic lifestyle, these settlements generated disturbing and divisive notions of wealth, territory, and ownership. As the communities proliferated, the amount of unused space diminished, personal rivalries increased, and competition—for land, for grain, for trade, for cattle, for labor—became the norm.

Even the most advanced societies were affected by the impulse to fight. The Assyrians, for example, who embellished much of the Middle East with their temples, palaces, and libraries, also became one of the world's foremost military powers. Other "civilized" powers have been hardly less bellicose in their relationships with their neighbors. The tiny city-states of Greece, though celebrated for their artists, poets, and philosophers, produced warriors who fought as ferociously against one another as they did against the common enemy of Persia. United in the fourth century BC under the warrior-kings of Macedonia, Philip II and his son Alexander the Great, Greek soldiers blazed a path of victory from the Mediterranean to the Indus River and from the Caucasus to the Red Sea.

Greece was succeeded in turn by another military colossus of the Mediterranean—Rome. By the year 250 BC, the Romans were well on the way to controlling the entire Italian peninsula: Over the next three centuries, the Roman legions—perhaps the best-trained soldiers in history—were to advance their battle standards throughout three continents, extending the Pax Romana to cover almost two million square miles of the earth's surface.

The Roman peace held throughout the Mediterranean and western Europe until the fourth century AD. But then the situation changed dramatically. The Huns—wild, nomadic horsemen from central Asia, who rode into battle at a gallop, raining arrows with devastating accuracy—began moving westward in search of grazing for their flocks. As these terrifying warriors approached, other barbarian peoples, such as the Visigoths and Ostrogoths, fled before them to push against the frontiers of the Roman world. The pressures proved irresistible, and in AD 410, with the legions beaten and scattered, the barbarians sacked Rome itself.

It was the start of a new era in the West, militarily as well as politically. Both the Greeks and the Romans had relied mainly on infantry, but the battlefield was now increasingly dominated by the mounted warrior—who would maintain ascendancy until the fifteenth century and the advent of several potent new weapons, including the gun. Indeed, gunpowder was to give the largely despised foot soldier a destructive capacity unsurpassed by a whole host of armored cavalry.

As war became progressively more lethal, it also grew increasingly costly, devouring more and more resources and manpower. Charles VIII of France, for example, invaded Italy in 1494 with a force of 18,000 soldiers; a little more than three centuries later, Napoleon Bonaparte marched into Russia with his so-called *Grande Armée* made up of 600,000 troops. After six months, the Grande Armée, harried not only by the Russian partisans but also by the Russian winter, had been reduced to some 60,000. Yet these losses seem small in comparison to those suffered by the warring powers of the twentieth century.

The hundred years following Napoleon's defeat saw unprecedented advances in the technology of annihilation: tanks, machine guns, long-range artillery, airplanes, submarines—all to be used in the great conflagration of 1914-1918 at a cost of more than 10 million lives. Barely a generation later, the leading powers were again at one another's throats—this time fighting on a truly global scale with weapons that were capable of destroying not just armies but entire populations. The climax came in 1945, when the United States dropped nuclear bombs on the Japanese cities of Hiroshima and Nagasaki.

After the common enemy was defeated, the wartime alliance between the West and the Soviet Union quickly collapsed, and the world entered the age of the paralyzed giants known as the Cold War. Held in check by the balance of nuclear terror, the two superpowers settled for a sullen and uneasy stalemate. Even so, this did not prevent hostilities from breaking out between nonnuclear powers. Africa, Asia, Latin America, the Middle East—all of these areas were scenes of prolonged and bloody conflicts, some caused by local rivalries, but many promoted, financed, and sustained by the Cold War antagonists.

Fought with an Aladdin's cave of sophisticated military hardware that ranged from hand-held missile launchers to helicopter gunships, these so-called limited wars would have astonished and appalled the Roman legionary—yet their savagery would have been all too familiar to a veteran of the siege of Carthage. For no matter how sweeping the technological changes, the essence of warfare is killing, and its chief practitioner has always been that most celebrated and vilified of historical figures—the front-line soldier.

It was the hot, alluvial lowlands of Mesopotamia, between the Tigris and Euphrates rivers, that first felt the tread of marching hosts. Here, around 10,000 BC, humans began the extraordinary transition from food gathering to food producing. The new lifestyle, which gradually spread through the rest of the Middle East and the Mediterranean, brought new opportunities—as well as new dangers. Conflict resulted when the possessors sought either to increase their lands and wealth at the expense of their neighbors or to defend what they had against the nonpossessors. Initially, those who fought were ordinary members of the community, mobilized for a particular emergency and serving under an elected leader who was distinguished by his competence and courage. As this early form of democracy yielded to the institution

A Mesopotamian soldier takes aim with his sling in this stone carving dating from the tenth century BC. The sling was made up of a pad, usually leather, that was attached to two thongs; the slinger would place a stone in the pad and then build up momentum by whirling the sling above his head before dispatching the stone toward its target. The sling remained one of the most lethal weapons in the infantry's armory even after the development of metallurgy. A skilled slinger could hit a mark up to 650 feet distant—a sharpened stone could pierce both clothing and flesh, while a blunt projectile could stun, smash bones, or even kill.

of kingship, however, a specialized class of professional warriors developed, owing allegiance to a hereditary ruler rather than to the community. Little is known about the organization or fighting techniques of these embryonic armies, but cave paintings demonstrate that they were familiar with the two basic tactical formations of the line and the column, and that they had learned how to carry out flanking maneuvers.

Life was made still more hazardous in the tenth millennium BC by the appearance of two powerful new weapons: the bow and the sling. For some 70,000 years, the principal means of dispatching quarry, animal or human, had been the spear. A versatile weapon, it could be used for either thrusting or throwing, and with its wooden shaft topped with a needle-sharp point of flint or bone, it was capable of penetrating the toughest hide. The simple bow, however, which consisted of a flexible length of wood and a string made of gut, introduced a dramatic increase in firepower. Its range of about 330 feet was double that of the spear. In addition, a single attacker was capable of carrying many more arrows than spears. Even deadlier than the bow was the leather sling, which could hurl bone-crushing missiles—stones and spherical shot of baked clay—more than 600 feet.

It was vital to seek protection against these long-range weapons, and settlements had to be as much fortified sanctuaries as convenient, comfortable dwelling places. One of the earliest known settlements, Jericho, founded in the Jordan Valley sometime before 8000 BC, was surrounded by both a deep ditch and a stone wall about ten feet thick and thirteen feet high. Extra security was provided by at least one stone tower, more than thirty feet in diameter and almost thirty feet high, that could be ascended by an internal stairway. (Such were the ramparts, according to the biblical story, that would succumb in the thirteenth century BC to the marching, shouting, and trumpeting host of Joshua and the Israelites.)

Farther north, at Çatal Hüyük in central Turkey, the square, mud-brick houses of the local farming community were built side by side without doors or windows. Access to each house was by means of a hatch in the roof from which a ladder led down into the living area. In the event of an attack, the ladders would be withdrawn by the occupants, and the enemy would be left facing a series of blank, solid walls. As fortifications improved, so did weaponry. The biggest impact came with the dawning of the age of metal. Bronze, which was first used for making artifacts about 3000 BC, had none of the brittleness of stone and was easily fashioned not only into hard, durable points and sharp-edged blades but also into shields, helmets, and scale armor. Iron, introduced approximately 1,500 years later, was even stronger than bronze, once the metalworkers discovered the technique of carbonized hardening. As a result of the mass production of high-quality weapons, war could now be waged on a scale and with a deadliness far exceeding anything that had gone before.

Another far-reaching innovation was the war chariot. First used in Mesopotamia around 3000 BC, the chariot was, in its earliest form, a clumsy, solid-wheeled wagon, drawn by asses rather than horses—more suitable for transporting the aristocratic warrior to the battlefield than for charging the enemy lines. Improvements continued, however, and by the eighteenth century BC, the spoked-wheel, lightweight war chariot, drawn by horses and combining speed with maneuverability, had become the clenched fist on the military forearm.

Chariot crews consisted of as many as four warriors, a driver and one or more javelin throwers or archers, the latter armed with the high-power composite bow. This was formed from a flat wooden strip covered with a layer of animal sinew on the outer side and long slivers of bone on the inner. As the bow was drawn, the sinew was stretched and the bone compressed, which gave it a far greater tension and velocity than that of the simple bow. In trained hands, it had an effective range of up to 900 feet. Measuring about four feet, it was also shorter than the simple bow and, so, was easier to fire from a fast-moving chariot.

But although chariots might inflict serious damage on the enemy infantry lines, they were rarely decisive. It was the clash of the two armies, striking and thrusting in hand-to-hand combat, that usually determined the winners and losers. Around 1483 BC, outside the city of Megiddo in Palestine, in one of the earliest recorded battles, the Egyptian ruler Tuthmosis III used his chariots to shatter the ranks of the opposing Canaanites. Instead of following up their success, however, the Egyptians paused to loot the enemy camp—countless armies over the ages would follow their example—allowing many of the enemy to escape into Megiddo itself. As a result, Tuthmosis had to lay siege to the city, which was starved into surrendering after seven months.

Warfare had by now become endemic throughout the Middle East, as its leading powers—Babylonians, Egyptians, Hurrians, Mitannians, Hittites, Kassites, Elamites, Amorites—struggled for supremacy. None of these peoples were to pursue this objective with more skill, dedication, or ferocity than the Assyrians. A farming and trading people whose earliest capital, Assur, had been founded during the third millennium BC on the banks of the Tigris River in northern Mesopotamia, the Assyrians had soon learned the hard lessons of war. As a consequence of its geographical position, the Assyrian kingdom became the constant target of envious and ambitious neighbors, and over the centuries, it experienced both triumph and defeat.

Protected by a copper helmet from blows to the head, a soldier depicted in a Sumerian plaque of the third millennium BC grips two of the earliest types of offensive weapons made of metal. In his right hand is an ax designed for piercing rather than chopping: A wooden haft slots into the socket of a rounded, sharp-edged blade. In his left hand, the soldier holds a sickle sword, fashioned from a single bar of metal, which he would use against his enemies as a farmer scythed grain.

The lowest ebb in the nation's fortunes came at the end of the eleventh century BC, when nomadic invaders from the north, the east, and the west rampaged through Assyrian territory. It was gradually squeezed into a narrow strip along the Tigris River barely 100 miles long and 50 miles wide. It emerged from this tiny enclave toward the end of the tenth century BC, however, to amass an empire that would ultimately stretch from the Nile Valley in Egypt almost as far as the Caucasus in Armenia—a distance of nearly 1,000 miles.

Such vast territories could not be conquered and comfortably governed without the presence of an effective army, and the military machine that was developed over the centuries by the Assyrians was awesome in both its size and its smooth-running complexity. Since troops could be called up at home as well as levied by local governors in conquered provinces, strength in sheer manpower could be enormous: A governor during the eighth century BC contributed 1,500 cavalrymen and 20,000 archers from his province for a single campaign. With more than twenty such provinces to draw on, the numbers raised by the Assyrians in a total mobilization would have been astronomical.

In practice, this was unlikely ever to happen: The limited, local operations that inevitably made up the main part of the army's work called for far smaller numbers. While armies more than 100,000 strong might be fielded for major campaigns, the Assyrians never relied on sheer weight of numbers for victory. Theirs was a carefully structured force with a range of specialized units that equipped it for every eventuality, from a large-scale pitched battle to the storming of a city.

At the heart of this army was a corps of professional, highly trained troops who acted not only as bodyguards to the king in his capital but also as his local garrison in important provincial cities. Very much the king's men, these soldiers answered to him rather than to the governor in whose province they happened to be serving. In addition to their peacetime duties, these crack troops could be expected to play a crucial role in battle, both guarding the king and helping to spearhead his attack. And since Assyrian rulers very determinedly led from the front, these two tasks amounted to much the same thing.

Although the Assyrians were the first major power to use horsemen as combatants rather than simply as messengers, it was the war chariot that gave their onslaught its explosive force. After an opening hail of iron-tipped arrows from the Assyrian archers had created the necessary confusion, the chariots would charge into the center of the enemy infantry while the cavalry encircled them on the wings. This twofold blow delivered in the first moments of battle was enough to break the spirit of most opponents, but it still had to be followed through. This was the task of the rank-and-file warriors conscripted from every part of the empire.

The Assyrians, though strict disciplinarians, made no attempt to mold their foreign troops into one approved training pattern. Instead, tolerant of local identities, they allowed contingents from the different regions to retain their own traditional clothing, weaponry, and style of fighting. Hence, they had at their disposal a highly versatile force comprising archers, slingers, swordsmen, pikemen, and both light and heavy infantrymen armed with spears. Just as important, it was an army whose troops retained their self-respect and, consequently, their morale.

In addition to these specialized combat formations, there were troops trained and equipped to provide technical backup. A pioneer corps armed with axes and sledge-hammers went ahead of an Assyrian army on the march to beat a track through difficult terrain so that the advancing columns, and the ox- and horse-drawn supply wagons at the rear, might progress without unnecessary delay. Where rivers or streams were encountered, the pioneers built rafts—inflating the skins of sheep and goats and using them to buoy up frameworks of wood and reeds—or joined rows of boats with planks to form pontoon bridges.

King Sargon II, writing about a campaign in 714 BC, described the rough passage his army experienced in crossing a tributary of the Tigris River when it was in full flood. They pushed on into "high mountains, covered with all kinds of trees, whose surface was a jungle, whose passes were frightful, over whose area shadows stretch as in a cedar forest, the traveler of whose paths never sees the light of the sun." Since such terrain was "too rough for chariots to mount, bad for horses, and too steep to march for foot soldiers," Sargon's pioneers "shattered the side of the high mountain as blocks of building stone, making a good road."

The pioneer and transportation divisions, which were so important in facilitating the speedy passage of the army, were also crucial in moving and operating its great siege engines—for the Assyrians were masters of siege warfare, devising techniques that would continue to be employed until well into the Middle Ages. Their sappers constructed ramps of earth and rubble in order to gain access to the upper and more vulnerable sections of a city's walls. Up these ramps would be hauled the heavy battering rams, huge metal-tipped logs, which were often mounted on wheels (although they were sometimes simply carried by teams of strong men) and housed in hide-covered wooden frames as protection against enemy missiles.

Scaling ladders and wheeled siege towers would also be used. The siege towers, made of wood and, similar to the battering rams, covered in a protective layer of hide, had platforms from which the Assyrian archers could fire down on those who were defending the walls. In areas where the city lay by a river, the siege towers would be floated into position from launching sites that were located safely upstream. While the enemy was thus engaged aboveground, the Assyrian engineers would be busy belowground, tunneling under the fortifications. The roofs of the tunnels were propped up with wooden supports, which would then be set on fire and brought crashing down—along with a section of the city wall.

Fire was an important weapon for besiegers and besieged alike, although it was a rather unpredictable one, since it was all too liable to turn on its user if carelessly handled or if a change of wind sent it in the wrong direction. Blazing arrows—so-called messengers of death—were shot into embattled cities, while crude petroleum, which seeped naturally from the ground in many parts of the Middle East, was sometimes ignited in order to create a wall of billowing flame around a siege site. The defenders, for their part, would throw torches or pour burning oil onto the besetting siege engines. These rarely had much effect, however, since the Assyrians always had men standing by ready to negate the effort by dousing the engines with water.

If a city's defenses appeared particularly strong, the Assyrians would probably avoid expending their forces in a direct attack: Instead, they would surround the city with a rough earthen rampart, post guards to prevent traffic in or out, and then simply wait for hunger to do their work for them. In the meantime, dire threats of the fate that awaited those who refused to surrender, and enticing promises of food and leniency for those who gave themselves up, assisted famine in sapping the defenders' morale.

The importance of psychology in warfare was well known to the Assyrians, who employed it with outstanding success. Atrocities were committed against rebellious peoples with a cynical eye to dissuading others. Lands were laid waste and cities burned, the inhabitants—men, women, and children alike—being slaughtered by the thousands; captives were horribly mutilated, flayed, and burned to death—all to drive home the same, simple message: Resistance to the power of Assyria did not pay.

King Sennacherib, having conquered the great city of Babylon in 689 BC, exulted in the carnage he had caused:

> Like the oncoming of a storm I broke loose and overwhelmed it like a hurricane. . . . With their corpses I filled the city squares. . . . The city and its houses, from its foundations to its top, I destroyed, I devastated, I burned with fire. The wall and outer wall, temples and gods, temple towers of brick and earth, as many as there were, I razed and dumped them into the Arahtu Canal. Through the midst of that city I dug canals, I flooded its site with water, and the very foundations thereof I destroyed. . . . That in days to come the site of that city, and its temples and gods, might not be remembered, I completely blotted it out with floods of water and made it like a meadow.

This was no simple blood lust—many of those attempting to flee from a devastated city were often permitted to do so, on the safe assumption that they would carry the news of what they had witnessed to neighboring cities and thus spread far and wide a paralyzing terror of Assyrian might. Mass deportations of civilian populations from their native areas to other parts of the empire—it has been estimated that between the tenth and seventh centuries BC, some four to five million people were moved in this way—also helped to instill fear and to break up organized resistance. The victims included 27,000 inhabitants of the kingdom of Israel who, carried off in 721 BC to eastern Syria, became the legendary ten lost tribes. On a more immediately practical level, such deportations provided pools of labor for major building and agricultural projects in underpopulated areas of Assyria and the empire.

Powerful as Assyria was at its zenith, it could not endure indefinitely. At the end of the seventh century BC, an alliance of neighboring states finally succeeded in defeating its armies and, in 612 BC, in sacking the imperial capital of Nineveh. After hundreds of years of dominance in the Middle East, Assyria's fall was comparatively abrupt. Its authority in the region was inherited first by a resurgent Babylon and then by the Persians who, though unrelated to the Assyrians, were the inheritors of their military organization and strategy. Long after Assyria had become a distant memory, through the sixth and fifth centuries BC, Assyrian ways of war were enabling the Persians to conquer their own vast empire, which stretched from the borders of India to the coasts of Turkey.

As the Persians prepared to expand their empire by moving farther to the west toward Greece, the Greek city-states were creating new forms of government, and

The central decoration of this third-century-BC Italian dish shows a young and a mature Indian elephant, the latter surmounted by a howdah—or crenelated tower—containing two warriors. Employed principally by Indian and Asian armies as living tanks, elephants caused cavalry horses to stampede in panic and terrified foot soldiers who had never seen these awe-inspiring beasts before. When an elephant got out of control, however, it could cause as much destruction among its own ranks as among the enemy. Poison-tipped scimitars were sometimes tied to the tusks, while archers rained down arrows from the fortified howdahs. An effective defense against elephants was to plant sharp spikes in the ground that pierced the soft soles of the animals' feet.

with them a new style of warfare—a style that would give their own armed forces, which were undermanned and seemingly outclassed, the ability to check the advancing tide of Persia's numberless armies. Through the early centuries of the first millennium BC, the local warlords who ruled the scattered villages of Greece had seen their power progressively eroded as increased trade in the Mediterranean region fostered a new class of commercial magnates—master craftsmen and independent farmers—whose wealth was soon rivaling that of the aristocracy, and whose loyalty was not to a noble but to their own particular community, embodied in the nascent city-state. It was inevitable that this new and powerful citizenry should endeavor to abolish the aristocracy's monopoly of military might and replace it with a system more suited to their own needs and interests.

Their triumphant answer, developed during the seventh and sixth centuries BC, was the hoplite phalanx. Hoplite soldiers—who were named after the heavy, circular wooden shield that was held rigidly by means of a distinctive double handle comprising a hoop in the center through which the arm was thrust to the elbow and a

handgrip at the rim—were citizens, serving alongside fellow citizens to protect the interests of their common state.

Military service, undertaken without pay, was a mark of full membership in the community, an essential prerequisite to participation in its decision making, and all those who could afford to do so—probably about one-third of the free adult males, or 8,000 men in a major city-state—bought the shield and the other basic equipment of the hoplite. This included long bronze greaves that protected the shins and calves; a bronze breastplate; a great bronze helmet, with a horsehair crest, that covered the neck and head, leaving only the eyes and mouth clear; a short, iron-bladed stabbing sword, used in emergencies; and an iron-pointed thrusting spear, some nine feet long, that was the hoplite's primary weapon.

The idea of communal dependence that had given rise to the hoplites was reflected in their tactics: They fought not as individuals but as a mass. The hoplites were, indeed, signally ill-suited to single combat. Their vision was restricted by cumbersome helmets, their movements inhibited by heavy armor, and their capacity to ward off any other than the most direct frontal attack limited by their weighty shields, whose rigid double grip prevented their use for deflecting angled blows. These weaknesses vanished, however, when the soldiers became part of the exactingly drilled, tightly knit battle formation known as the phalanx.

Standing literally shoulder to shoulder, each man getting his unprotected side as close as possible to the shield of the comrade on his right, the hoplites in their phalanx seemed to become a single entity. When two phalanxes clashed, each would try to bulldoze its way forward, those in the front rank on either side keeping their shields rigidly locked together with their left arms while, with their right, they delivered savage overarm spear thrusts to the head and neck. Only if their spears broke would hoplites use their swords—and then they would attempt to thrust beneath the rival shield wall to the groin and abdomen.

The aim was to keep the front rank solid so that there would be no gaps through which the enemy could penetrate. As hoplites in the leading line fell, those behind them crowded forward, trampling over the bodies of their comrades, to take their place. The encounters between these mobile human fortresses depended as much on brute strength as on courage, and the Greeks had an appropriate word for them— *othismos,* or "the shoving."

Within the confined space of Greece, with its limited natural resources, competition between the city-states was fierce, and warfare almost constant. These clashes tended to be somewhat ritualistic, however—trials mounted to establish which party in a dispute had the gods on its side—and a phalanx would claim victory if its opponents retreated, declining to press its advantage. In the early days of the city-states, indeed, disputes were often settled by individual champions or by teams of champions, fighting under strict rules.

According to the Greek historian Herodotus, one such contest took place as late as 546 BC, between 300 soldiers from Argos and 300 from Sparta. The outcome was supposed to determine which of the two cities was entitled to the disputed territory of Thyrea. If Herodotus is to be believed, however, the engagement ended with both sides claiming victory—the Spartans because their one survivor had remained on the battlefield, the Argives because their two survivors, though having left the field, outnumbered their lone rival. Unable to agree, the two sides then plunged into a full-scale battle, which the Spartans won.

The supreme test of the hoplites came in 490 BC, with the invasion of mainland Greece by the Persian king Darius I. Darius had increased the Persian empire in the east to its farthest extent—beyond the Indus River and into the fringes of India itself—and was justifiably confident of being as successful in the west against the small, scattered armies of the Greeks. At Marathon, however, the forces of the Athenians and their allies, though outnumbered by almost two to one, fought back with a boldness and tenacity that astonished the Persians.

To reduce the amount of time his hoplites would be exposed to the Persian arrows, the Athenian commander Miltiades the Younger ordered them to advance on the double. According to Herodotus, the Persians thought it "suicidal madness for the Athenians to risk an assault with so small a force—rushing in with no support from either cavalry or archers." Pressed hard, bearing the brunt of a heavy Persian counterattack, the Greek center began to sag, but failed to break.

On the wings, meanwhile, where the Greeks were stronger, they broke the enemy line and swept inward from right and left to envelop the center. Hemmed in as they now were on three sides, the pride of Darius's army, including the cavalry, fled to its ships. For the first time, a Persian army that had previously carried all before it had been defeated. Herodotus, exaggerating only a little, wrote that the victors of Marathon were "the first Greeks . . . who dared to look without flinching at Persian dress and the men who wore it; for until that day came, no Greek could hear even the word

Persian without terror." The decisive clash came eleven years later at Plataea, where another vast Persian army was routed by the numerically inferior Greeks. Far greater defeats lay in store for the Persians, however.

During the fourth century BC, a Greece worn down by years of internecine warfare fell under the sway of a strongman from the mountains of the north—Macedonia's king Philip II—to be galvanized by his iron rule and re-created as an imperial power. Philip's toughness was legendary, and he insisted on physical endurance, hardness, and self-reliance in his soldiers: He stationed cavalry units behind the ranks of his infantry to kill any deserters and barred women altogether from the Macedonian camp. Philip's officers, unlike their Greek counterparts, were not allowed to ride in wagons during a campaign; instead, they had to march with their troops, even in the heat of summer. And where each Greek hoplite had his own personal servant to dress him for battle and tend to his other needs on the march, the Macedonians were permitted only one attendant for ten men.

A crucial role in Philip's army was played by the so-called Companions, a 3,000-strong detachment of heavy cavalry. Armed with the Macedonian cavalry lance, or *xyston,* an awesome weapon almost twelve feet long, with a twelve-inch iron point at both ends—the second point could be used for fighting if the first was broken off—these highly skilled horsemen were adept at drawing off hostile cavalry forces or charging into vulnerable sections of the enemy line. The stirrup was still unknown, and only rigorous training ensured that the Companions retained their mounts in the fury of close-quarter combat. They would normally charge with xystons held underarm, aiming for the enemy's face or horse's head. If they were fighting foot soldiers, the Companions would use their xystons overarm, striking downward.

The brunt of the battle was borne, however, by the Foot Companions, the Macedonian infantry. Some 24,000 in number, they carried a small, round shield that was strapped to the left shoulder, thus leaving both hands free to wield the *sarissa,* their own version of the cavalry lance. Instead of a second point, however, this weapon had a metal spike at the butt end so that it could be planted firmly in the ground and used to impale a charging horseman.

Drawn up in a phalanx sixteen ranks deep, with the sarissas of the first five ranks extending beyond the bodies of the soldiers in the front rank, the Foot Companions advanced on their opponents like a vast, menacing porcupine. But they were as meticulously drilled as their comrades in the cavalry and could quickly broaden their front, thinning out from behind, or, if surrounded, turn at a word of command to form a tight, outward-facing defensive square. Since, in their usual formation, the Foot Companions' right flank was relatively vulnerable, this was protected by an elite corps of 3,000 foot-soldiers, the Royal Shield Bearers, who were also used as a commando unit to spearhead attacks on entrenched enemy positions.

Around this solid core of Macedonians, Philip deployed not only the troops of his subject allies but also foreign mercenaries—archers, slingers, javelin throwers, cavalry—which gave him forces that were equal to any occasion. Confident of his military power, he decided to turn eastward to begin the conquest of Asia. In 336 BC, however, having landed a 10,000-strong advance guard in Asia Minor, Philip was assassinated, and the campaign was taken over by his son and successor, twenty-year-old Alexander. The army that Alexander had inherited from his father was perhaps the finest the world had yet seen—and he would prove himself more than worthy of leading it.

Assyrian chariots surge into battle in this ninth-century-BC stone relief. Each chariot is drawn by two horses—with a reserve third horse loosely attached to the reins in case of injury—and is crewed by a driver and an archer. Quivers of arrows are attached to the chariot's side; a shield and spear for the driver are secured at the rear. Swift, light, and maneuverable, chariots came into their own in the early and latter stages of a battle: They made darting attacks on an enemy formation while their own infantry advanced for the main assault, and they pursued retreating troops to complete a rout. A mass frontal attack generally succeeded only when the enemy troops lost their nerve and broke formation.

In 334 BC, after suppressing a wave of unrest that had arisen in the wake of his father's death, Alexander crossed over to Asia Minor with an army of 32,000 foot soldiers and 5,000 cavalrymen. Their first encounter with the Persians of Darius III, on the banks of the Granicus River, was to set the pattern of the next three years. Although the Persians fought valiantly, they were no match for the toughness, discipline, and tactical cunning of their opponents. A clever feint by Alexander drew part of the Persian cavalry out of its position in line, at which point he sent his own horsemen storming across the river to smash through the Persian center. In the debacle that followed, thousands of Greek mercenary hoplites in Darius's pay were surrounded and massacred. The total Macedonian losses were said to be 115.

In 333 BC, having secured all of Asia Minor, Alexander marched south into Syria, where Darius awaited him with an army at least twice as large as his own. They clashed near the town of Issus, on the Mediterranean coast. After a bitter struggle in which Darius's hoplites came close to cracking the Macedonian phalanx—a sweet revenge for the defeat at the Granicus—Alexander prevailed again. Darius's army was decisively beaten, and several members of his family were taken prisoner. Darius himself threw down his weapons and fled the field in panic.

Although the king sued for peace, offering to give up all his territories west of the Euphrates, Alexander refused to bargain: He was going to take the whole of Darius's domain—and without conditions. His first aim was to neutralize the huge Persian fleet by seizing its land bases on the Mediterranean—an exercise that would test the skills of his army in siege warfare.

The Greek engineers on Philip's staff had designed wheeled siege towers that were stronger and more sophisticated than any seen previously. Equipped with wide drawbridges that could be let down and used to gain access to enemy battlements, these towers had different levels from which specialists wielded bows, slings, crossbows, grappling irons, and battering rams. Philip's engineers had also developed the torsion catapult, a mechanism in which skeins of hair or sinew were twisted as tightly as possible and then allowed to spring free, the power being sufficient to hurl large rocks as far as 1,200 feet.

Despite such devices, however, it took Alexander six months to overcome the port of Tyre in Phoenicia (present-day Lebanon). The city finally fell when the Macedonians succeeded in breaching a section of its defensive wall. Outraged at the obstinate defiance of the Tyrians, Alexander's soldiers poured into the city and engaged in an orgy of killing and destruction. Tyre was burned, and 2,000 of its surviving inhabitants were crucified. Gaza, the second town to offer resistance, fell after two months, and in November 332 BC, Alexander entered Egypt in triumph. After being crowned pharaoh, the young conqueror turned his attention eastward once more, back to the Persian heartland.

At the end of the following summer, Alexander crossed the Euphrates River into Mesopotamia, where Darius, having assembled another enormous army, was prepared for the final showdown. This conflict took place on October 1, near the village of Gaugamela. In addition to his regular forces, the king was relying on a secret weapon—200 scythe chariots—which he believed would give him a decisive advantage in the coming battle. The notion of a chariot whose whirling axle blades would cut a bloody swath through the enemy ranks, reaping lives like ears of grain, was a potent one for leaders of the ancient world: A previous Persian king, Artaxerxes II, had experimented with scythe chariots approximately seventy years earlier, and the concept would resurface periodically until well into the time of the Romans.

In practice, the supposed superweapon was nearly always a miserable failure. Terrible though its blades may have been in theory, enemy soldiers avoided them simply by parting their ranks; then they pelted the chariot with missiles, seized its horses by their harness, brought the vehicle to a halt, and killed its single operator. (Sometimes a driver would jump clear of the speeding vehicle before it reached enemy lines, preferring the risk of broken bones to the certainty of a violent death.) So it was to prove at Gaugamela, where Darius's chariot charge was broken by the arrows and javelins of the Macedonians. Meanwhile, a well-placed, coordinated thrust from the Companions and Foot Companions tilted the battle in Alexander's favor. Soon the Persian center, commanded by Darius himself, was on the run, with Alexander's troops in pursuit.

With the victory of Gaugamela, Alexander had put an end to the power of the Persians. He went on quickly to occupy Babylon, then sacked and destroyed the imperial capital of Persepolis before marching after the fleeing Darius. The king was found by the wayside, dying of stab wounds, his throne having been seized by one of his vassals, Bessus. Alexander moved eastward, capturing and executing the usurper and fighting a tough guerrilla campaign against the inhabitants of the eastern satrapies. Finally, in 326 BC, he crossed the Hindu Kush into India. Here, by the turbulent Hydaspes River, he was confronted by the army of the Indian king Porus, complete with its own surprise weapon—200 elephants.

Long employed in Indian warfare, the elephant—draped with leather or quilted armor and painted with elaborate designs, its tusks capped with metal tips and strengthening rings—was typically crewed by a driver and a pair of javelin throwers or archers. The very sight of these massive, brightly decorated monsters, lumbering onto the battlefield like animated siege towers, was frequently sufficient to create panic and flight among the enemy, especially an enemy that was encountering the elephants for the first time.

Intimidating as these great beasts were, not even they could induce Alexander's forces to break ranks. Indeed, panicked by the cacophony of battle, the elephants blundered about blindly, trampling to death as many of the troops on their own side as those of the enemy. The day ended in a rout for the Indians, but Alexander was sufficiently impressed by Porus's courage and leadership to reinstate him as king under Macedonian overlordship.

After the victory at the Hydaspes, Alexander was anxious to push on deeper into India, but by now his troops were showing signs of outright rebellion. In the eight years since leaving their own shores, they had marched almost 17,000 miles, and they refused to go any farther. Reluctantly, Alexander agreed to lead them home, but he was destined never to see his native land again. On reaching Babylon, he was suddenly taken ill, probably with malaria, and died on June 10, 323 BC. The conqueror of western Asia, and arguably the greatest general the world has ever seen, was only thirty-two years old.

Alexander's death plunged the Hellenic world into a state of turmoil that lasted for several decades, as his generals warred among themselves for the succession to his crown, making one great battlefield of the vast territories he had conquered, from Persia to the Mediterranean. Yet the prize they were fighting for was dwindling in value year by year, as the competing forces razed the empire's cities, slaughtered its

Among peoples for whom battle was the supreme test of manhood, those who fought most gloriously achieved almost superhuman status. Over time, as their deeds were woven into legend and celebrated in ballads and folklore, the most famous national heroes—such as Gilgamesh of Mesopotamia, the Greek Achilles, or the French medieval warrior Roland—acquired many of the attributes of divinity. Yet, while some of them were invulnerable to human weapons and others possessed magical strength or skills, they were still mortal, their deaths a form of sacrifice to the gods whose capricious rule made war a natural condition of life on earth.

Proud, reckless, and resourceful, these straightforward warriors served as role models for all soldiers. And because each became identified with a particular people's mythology, their example perpetuated the martial rivalry among nations.

A sixth-century-BC vase painting shows the Greek warrior Achilles slaying Penthesileia, legendary queen of the Amazons. Dipped in the river Styx as a child, Achilles was vulnerable to mortal weapons only in his heel, where an arrow finally struck home during the Trojan War.

The Norse hero Sigurd— known in Teutonic legend as Siegfried—is shown in this twelfth-century woodcarving with the broken segments of a magical sword. His mending of the sword was the prelude to a series of heroic battles against both mortal and demonic adversaries.

This seventeenth-century miniature from the *Shah-nama*, a history of the legendary rulers of ancient Persia, celebrates the victory of the hero Rustem over his country's enemies. By means of this and other feats, Rustem secured the foundation of the Persian nation.

civilians, and laid waste its pastures. Less obviously, the struggle was becoming increasingly futile because Macedonia was soon to be eclipsed by a new military power already emerging across the Adriatic Sea in present-day Italy.

Since the eighth century BC, a settlement founded near the Tiber River—on the eastern side of the Italian peninsula—by a tribe of shepherds, known as the Latins, had been steadily growing in importance. At the end of the sixth century BC, the prominent citizens of Rome, as the city was now called, rose up in alliance with Greek settlers from nearby colonies to drive out their local overlords, the Etruscans, and declared a republic. The newly independent Rome then became leader of the Latin towns in an anti-Etruscan alliance, the Latin League. At first following the practice of their Etruscan rulers in using what was basically a Greek-style citizens' hoplite phalanx of heavy infantry armed with round shields and thrusting spears, the independent Romans soon began to modernize their army.

The wars that the Latin League went on to fight after the decline of Etruria, against other tribes of the Italian peninsula, made clear the limitations of the hoplite phalanx. It was too unwieldy to maneuver on the rough Italian terrain, and its flanks were highly vulnerable to attack by tribesmen using a loose and unpredictable battle style. At the beginning of the fourth century BC, therefore, the phalanx was abandoned in favor of a more flexible formation, the legion. Its numbers varied according to circumstance, but its basic tactical structure remained constant: three lines of foot soldiers drawn up according to age and experience. First came the youngest and least experienced, the *hastati;* next came their immediate seniors, the *principes,* aged about thirty and with several years' service; finally came the oldest group, the *triarii,* battle-hardened veterans whose steadiness and maturity helped to strengthen the morale of the less-seasoned troops.

Only the third line retained the spear, while the first and second lines were armed with the heavy javelin, or pilum. Measuring nine feet, it had a head of soft iron that was connected to the shaft by a slender neck. When struck home, the point became bent and the head usually broke off, thus making the weapon useless to the other side. In addition, the head would usually remain embedded in the enemies' shields and armor, which added greatly to their discomfort. After throwing their javelins, the hastati would draw swords and charge in for close combat. If the attack failed, the survivors would retreat through the ranks of the principes, who would then mount their own assault. In the event that both attacks failed, the survivors would retreat behind the triarii, who would then close ranks, level their spears, and provide a protective wall for a retreat to the safety of the camp.

In fact, retreat was rarely necessary, and by the end of the third century BC, Rome had subjugated the entire Italian peninsula. The Italian peoples were allowed to govern themselves as allies, although Rome retained control of their foreign policy. They were also subject to being conscripted for military service—and Rome was soon to need all the troops it could get. In the year 280 BC, King Pyrrhus of Epirus arrived in Italy from the Greek mainland with a sarissa phalanx and twenty war elephants. A brilliant general, Pyrrhus defeated the Romans in a series of battles, but at such a cost in casualties to his own troops that he was eventually forced to retreat before superior Roman numbers.

Rome was by this time clearly established as a major power, a fact that was to bring it into inevitable conflict with Carthage, the ruler of the western Mediterranean region, located in North Africa. Founded centuries earlier by Phoenician traders from the ports of Lebanon, Carthage had grown into a prosperous maritime empire embracing Corsica, Sardinia, Sicily, and Spain as well as North Africa. It brooked no rivals and regarded the rise of Rome with a suspicion and hostility that were fully reciprocated. The first of three wars against Carthage—the so-called Punic Wars, from *Punicus,* the Latin word for the Phoenicians—began in 264 BC, when Rome intervened in the affairs of Sicily.

This turned out to be primarily a naval conflict, which put the Romans, who had neither experience of nor enthusiasm for such warfare, at a serious disadvantage. Nevertheless, they set to work building a fleet. By a stroke of luck, they discovered a stranded Carthaginian war galley, and with the help of Greek naval architects, they made 100 copies of it in sixty days. They also added a refinement of their own—a combined boarding platform and grappling hook—nicknamed the *corvus,* or raven—that could be slammed onto the enemy deck, thus enabling the Roman legionaries to swarm across to engage in hand-to-hand fighting. But the Romans remained inexpert sailors, and they lost far more troops to the elements than they did to the Carthaginians. In 241 BC, however, after almost twenty-five years of continuous struggle, the Carthaginians were driven out of Sicily. Roman persistence and Roman personnel had prevailed.

In 218 BC, the Second Punic War broke out. This time, the fighting took place primarily on land, although this proved to be hardly an advantage to the Romans. Led by an outstanding general, Hannibal, the Carthaginians set out from southern Spain and marched east across the Pyrenees and the Alps to invade Italy itself. During the course of three successive battles—at the Trebbia River, at Lake Trasimeno, and at Cannae—the legions suffered total and humiliating defeat. At Cannae alone, they lost more than 45,000 soldiers.

The Romans, however, refused to give up. Their attitude was made clear in the reply given to Hannibal's ambassador after the battle at Cannae: "Rome will not discuss terms of peace with a foreign enemy on Italian soil." They now set about recovering their lost territories, retaking enemy-held cities one by one, and avoiding a direct encounter with Hannibal. It was a long war of attrition in which they were assisted by seemingly inexhaustible reserves of manpower: By 212 BC, Rome had 25 legions—almost 250,000 troops—in the field, a strength that Hannibal, fighting far from home and cut off from both reinforcements and supplies, could never hope to match. At last Rome counterattacked, landing an army in North Africa, and Hannibal hurried back to defend his homeland. He was defeated in 202 BC at the battle of Zama, near the Carthaginian capital.

Faced with near extinction only a few years earlier, Rome had not only emerged triumphant but had also laid the foundations of its overseas empire. Strength of numbers, flexible tactics, and appropriate weaponry had all contributed to this achievement, but the might of Rome depended above all on the quality and loyalty of the individual soldiers who composed the legions. As the Greek commander Xenophon had reminded his troops some 200 years earlier, when they appeared disheartened by the weapons and horses of the enemy they faced, "it is men who do whatever gets done in battle."

The technique of turning raw recruits into a well-disciplined fighting force was by no means a Roman monopoly, but in this particular society the system had become so efficient that it seemed a natural process of life. The army was the linchpin of the state: All male citizens between the ages of seventeen and forty-five were obliged to serve for at least ten years, and anyone with political ambitions had first to prove his worth as a soldier. To be declared unfit to serve was to be disgraced and to forsake all hope of public employment.

The learning of obedience to authority began in early childhood, for in the family home, the father was an absolute autocrat with the power of life and death over his sons. Thus, when a boy first donned the soldier's outfit of woolen tunic and hobnailed sandals, he was already conditioned to obey commands without question. And in case this lesson had not been fully learned, the young recruit faced severe penalties if he stepped out of line. The historian Tacitus recorded an incident in which two soldiers working on a fortification were executed for not wearing their swords as regulations demanded. A law passed as early as 449 BC prescribed the death penalty—administered by scourging for common soldiers, and by beheading for officers—for a range of offenses from mutiny to failing to keep proper order in battle. Punishments for lesser misdemeanors included whipping with rods and running the gantlet between fellow soldiers who stoned and beat the luckless offender. In cases of collective disobedience, the military authorities could order the savage penalty of decimation—the execution of every tenth man in a legion.

The threat rather than the actual imposition of such punishments was usually sufficient to enforce discipline, for by the time a recruit had undergone his basic training, any willful spirit of insubordination was likely to have been eradicated. Legionaries trained systematically in the handling of weapons, practiced athletic activities such as running, jumping, and weightlifting to develop their physiques, and underwent a punishing daily routine of marching, drilling, and maneuvering that was no mere playacting. "Their battle drills are no different from the real thing," marveled the Jewish chronicler Josephus at the end of the first century AD. "Every man works as hard at his daily training as if he were on active service. That is why they stand up so easily to the strain of battle. . . . It would not be far from the truth to call their drills bloodless battles, their battles bloody drills." Similarly strict discipline extended into all areas of the legionary's life. "They do not have supper or breakfast just when they fancy at their individual discretion, but all together. Time for sleep, guard duty, and reveille are announced by trumpet calls, and nothing whatever is done without orders."

While they were engaged in a campaign, soldiers were inspired by the possibilities of booty and other rewards. The psychology of military training was well understood: "Punishment and fear thereof are necessary to keep soldiers in quarters," declared

Slaves—probably the most valuable form of war booty in the ancient world—are shown in this stone relief tramping up a steep incline to contribute their burden of stones to the building of the palace of King Sennacherib, ruler of Assyria at the start of the seventh century BC. In Assyria, Egypt, and other early states, all captives belonged first to the king and were used chiefly as forced labor in the construction of public works such as forts, canals, and royal palaces. Vassal kingdoms were also required to supply slave-soldiers to "fight and even die for the king," in the words of one Assyrian edict. By the time of the Romans, slaves were sold at markets for employment in private households.

one Roman general, "but in the field, they are more influenced by hope and rewards." In recognition of outstanding conduct in battle, a soldier might be awarded one of a number of official decorations that included medallions and special armbands and collars. A crown, or the *corona muralis,* was the prize for the first soldier to scale the walls of a besieged town. For a victorious commander, the supreme recognition of valor was a triumphal procession: Dressed in a purple and gold tunic, the general rode in a chariot through the streets of Rome at the head of a column that included hostages, prisoners, and a display of booty. The resounding acclaim of the Roman citizenry was the ultimate seal of approval.

In this seventh-century-BC stone relief, Assyrian scribes holding a scroll and a hinged writing board make an inventory of items captured from a Chaldean settlement south of the Euphrates River. The stacked booty includes daggers, quivers, and a bundle of composite bows, as well as a bed and other furniture. The lure of booty was a powerful incitement for kings and common soldiers alike; if its distribution was not strictly controlled, however, discipline was liable to break down. An Egyptian chronicle of the second millennium BC records an occasion when a city might have been captured "if only His Majesty's army had not given up their hearts to capturing the possessions of the enemy."

The pride and discipline instilled in the Roman soldier were to sustain his loyalty through tests of boredom, climate, disease, and hunger, as well as battle. Pacing the frontier wall in the icy winds of northern England or marching across the searing desert sands of Syria, most legionaries doubtless daydreamed of the comforts of home, but few absconded from their lot. Their very presence in these remote regions bolstered their self-esteem, for it demonstrated the superiority of their own civilization to those that they had conquered and annexed.

This confidence derived from a series of military victories, which in turn were made possible by the adoption of improved weapons and tactics. Notice was first served that a new imperial power was in the ascendant, with a new way of war, by the Roman defeat of Philip V's Macedonian phalanx at Cynoscephalae in Thessaly in 197 BC. By now, the legionary's main combat weapon was the *gladius hispaniensis,* or Spanish sword, probably introduced to Italy by troops who had fought against the Carthaginians in Spain. A broad-bladed, double-edged sword some 2.3 feet long, designed mainly for thrusting, it was the terror of Rome's enemies. According to the Roman historian Livy, the Greeks, with experience only of javelin, spear, and arrow wounds, were horrified at the mutilations this type of sword caused: "When they had seen bodies chopped to pieces . . . arms torn away, shoulders and all, heads separated from bodies with the necks completely severed, and stomachs ripped open, they realized in a general panic with what weapons, and what men, they had to fight."

Seven years after Cynoscephalae, the Romans defeated Antiochus the Great of Syria to become the undisputed rulers of the Mediterranean region. Over the next century, they were to score many more such triumphs, including the final destruction of Carthage in 146 BC, following the Third Punic War. As its empire expanded, however, and more and more troops were needed for foreign campaigning, Rome

The remains of triple lines of ramparts and ditches surround the site of Maiden Castle in Dorset, southern England. Constructed around 4,000 years ago, this hill fort—covering an area of 160 acres—provided a safe haven for the people of nearby villages in time of danger. Passage to the main entrance in the inner rampart—at the bottom right of this aerial photograph—was impeded by overlapping outer ramparts. During an attack, the entrance itself was probably blocked by boulders or tree trunks.

On the crest of a steep promontory jutting from the coast of New Zealand, a Maori village is surrounded by a high timber palisade. From a platform erected on the top of the fence, defenders could fire arrows at attackers scaling the hillside. This painting was executed in 1769 by an artist accompanying the British navigator Captain Cook, who noted that the villagers in such stockades prepared themselves for a siege by laying in supplies of fern roots, dried fish, and fresh water in gourds.

SAFE HAVENS

Early human communities soon learned that the more successful they were in producing wealth, the more attractive a target they became for raiders from outside their borders. In order to survive, they had to invest in communal defenses.

An elevated location was the first requirement: From the summit of a hill, a lookout could warn fellow citizens of an approaching enemy. A summit also offered a strategic bonus to the defenders, enabling them to rain down missiles on the attackers as they labored up the hillside. To capitalize on these advantages, hilltops were surrounded with earthen ramparts and parallel ditches. Where wood was abundant, the ramparts might be supplemented or replaced by timber stockades.

But a hilltop was unlikely to be blessed with fresh water, essential if the community was to endure a prolonged siege, and timber fortifications could be set on fire. Therefore, from the time of Jericho and Troy, no prosperous city was built without a massive encircling wall of stone.

Solid stone defenses that protected the Greek city of Aigósthena at the eastern end of the Gulf of Corinth date from the fourth century BC. The projecting towers built at regular intervals along the wall allowed defenders to cross fire on attackers attempting to scale the walls or dig beneath them.

This map shows the extent of the Roman Empire in the second century AD and the main towns in which Roman legions were garrisoned. For Rome—as for all other imperial powers—the problems of securing such far-flung frontiers and safeguarding trade routes posed extreme administrative and logistic challenges. The legions numbered around 160,000 and were widely dispersed; the borders were defended mostly by locally recruited auxiliaries. Where it was possible to do so, Rome established friendly relations with states between its provinces and a potential aggressor, but diplomacy could succeed only if backed by military strength. Because of the distance over which they stretched, the forts and walls built in vulnerable zones could check but not withstand a major enemy incursion. More than on manpower alone, Rome relied on the deterrent effect of its military reputation—as demonstrated by the detail (right) of a second-century-AD milestone from the Antonine Wall in Britain that shows a Roman horseman riding down a group of native rebels.

BRITAIN
York.
. Chester
. Caerleon

Atlantic Ocean

Xanten. **GERMANY**
Bonn.
. Mainz

Strasbourg . *Danube River*
FRANCE Vienna
Cornutum . Szony
. Budapest

. Karlsburg

. León
Belgrade . Troesmis
ITALY . Silistra *Black Sea*
Viminacium . Nevae
SPAIN . Rome

Caspian Sea

. Kelkit

TURKEY . Malatya

. Sura

. Lambèse *Mediterranean Sea*
Raphana
. Busra
. Jerusalem
. Alexandria

NORTH AFRICA

EGYPT

Red Sea

found it increasingly difficult to meet its personnel needs. The property qualification, though still an official requirement for military service, tended to be ignored, and growing numbers of the rural landless and urban poor made up the fighting force.

Lacking a strong identification with the state and with no social position to maintain, the new breed of soldier did not have quite the same stake in the empire's future as his better-off colleagues, and discipline and morale suffered accordingly. Around 100 BC, therefore, the consul Gaius Marius introduced a series of reforms designed to get the best possible performance out of the new recruits. Marius, who was himself of humble origin, abolished the old militia-style army, replacing it with an organization of full-time military professionals whose first loyalty was to their commanders rather than to the government in Rome.

The system was a resounding success, and for two centuries, the Roman army pushed back the frontiers of the empire into northern and central Europe and the Middle East, seldom suffering more than temporary reverses. Throughout this period, the primary threat to the empire came from within its borders, as the legions marched against one another to support the claims to power of rival generals. In 44 BC, Julius Caesar, the conqueror of Gaul, brought several years of political ferment to a head when he had himself appointed dictator for life—and was promptly assassinated. The civil wars that followed Caesar's death continued for more than a decade and almost tore the empire apart.

Somehow, through all the turmoil, it endured; and when in 27 BC, Octavius, Julius Caesar's heir, at last emerged as undisputed ruler of Rome and was hailed as the emperor Augustus, a new era of internal peace began. The army was now free to begin conquering fresh territory, and by the second century AD, Rome's domain stretched from Scotland to the Sahara, from Portugal to Palestine.

The empire's prosperity acted as a magnet to barbarian tribes, however, who pressed increasingly on its boundaries. In AD 293, in an effort to make the realm more defensible, the emperor Diocletian divided it into two parts—the east, which he ruled from Nicomedia in Asia Minor, and the west, ruled by a coemperor in Milan. Early in the fourth century, the emperor Constantine established a new eastern capital, Constantinople (now Istanbul). It would take more than administrative juggling to avert the approaching deluge, however.

In the 370s, the Huns, a nomadic people from central Asia, began to sweep westward in search of fresh pastures for their great flocks of sheep and goats and their herds of horses. Expert horsemen and fearless warriors, their faces ritually scarred and tattooed with fierce animals and dragons, these invaders galloped toward their terrified enemy shooting light but penetrating bone-tipped arrows from short composite bows. The Roman soldier-historian Ammianus Marcellinus saw these warriors in action and wrote of them:

> *When they join battle, they advance in packs, uttering their various war cries. Being lightly equipped and very sudden in their movements, they can deliberately scatter and gallop about at random, inflicting tremendous slaughter; their extreme nimbleness enables them to force a rampart or pillage an enemy's camp before one catches sight of them. . . . At close quarters, they fight without regard for their lives, and while their opponents are guarding against sword thrusts, they catch their limbs in lassos of twisted cloth that make it impossible for them to ride or walk.*

The Huns inspired terror even among neighboring nomadic peoples such as the warlike Ostrogoths and Visigoths, who poured westward themselves, starting a chain reaction of panicked flight. By the year 376, almost 250,000 Germanic tribe members had swarmed across the empire's Danube frontier. After being mistreated by grasping and incompetent Roman officials, they began to roam the countryside at will, killing, burning, and looting. In the spring of 378, an army led by the emperor Valens marched out of Constantinople to confront them.

The invaders, led by the Visigoth chieftain Fritigern, had set up their camp—an immense circle of fortified wagons—near Adrianople, and it was here that Valens's army duly arrived on August 9. The legionaries, though exhausted after a long morning's march in the broiling sun, were ordered by the emperor to launch an immediate attack. As they advanced toward the Visigoth wagons, however, thousands of enemy horsemen, returning from a foraging expedition, suddenly swept down on them from the high ground to their right. The legions were still struggling to hold off this onslaught when they were charged by the infantry from the camp. The battle quickly became a slaughter. The emperor, his leading generals, and 40,000 of his soldiers were killed. Not since Cannae, almost 600 years earlier, had the Romans suffered such a shattering defeat.

The city of Rome itself was sacked by the Visigoths in 410 and by the Vandals in 455. Still, the western empire lingered on, making deals with the invaders, playing off one group against another, even recruiting them into the legions. Indeed, the number of barbarians marching behind the standards of Rome gradually came to exceed the number of Romans. For the most part, such soldiers had loyalty to neither the state nor the army, both of which continued to decline. The deathblow came in 476, when the army's Germanic mercenaries deposed the emperor Romulus Augustulus and proclaimed their chief, Odoacer, king. The Roman Empire in the east would endure for another millennium, even reconquering for a time some of the western provinces. But the empire in the west was finished forever. Its power had depended on the skill, courage, and sheer footslogging determination of the legions. Now they, too, were gone, and in the military age just dawning, it was to be the mounted warrior who reigned supreme.

As Confederate troops charged the enemy lines during the American Civil War, they uttered a piercing scream that came to be known as the rebel yell. "There is nothing like it on this side of the infernal region," recalled a Union soldier. "The peculiar corkscrew sensation that it sends down your back . . . can never be told."

As all successful military commanders have known, in convincing an enemy to capitulate, terror may be no less effective than superior numbers or arms. In some cases, it may be the single most important factor. In Mexico in 1519, for example, the Spanish conquistador Hernán Cortés and his 500 men were surrounded by several thousand hostile warriors. Cortés invited the enemy chiefs to his tent, where he pa-

raded before them an excited stallion, and then ordered a cannon to be fired. The terrified Mexican Indians, who had never seen a horse or cannon before, meekly submitted to the foreign invader.

The Viking marauders who devastated coastal settlements in western Europe in the ninth and tenth centuries equipped their ships with, in the words of a Norse poet, "grim gaping heads" such as that shown on the left. These functioned as protective charms for the crew and as terror-magic for the enemy. Other examples of some of the most basic means of inducing panic are shown on the following pages. They include body decoration and clothing designed to make soldiers appear as invulnerable demons as well as the use of noise—such as battle cries or drums—to further dishearten an opponent. Secret weapons unfamiliar to an enemy—such as elephants used in battle or the first tanks in World War I—have also had a psychological impact out of all proportion to the actual damage they caused.

Of more long-term effect was the deliberate use of atrocities to enhance a reputation for ferocity and intimidate an enemy even before battle was joined. In the thirteenth century, for example, the Mongols massacred the entire citizenry of towns that dared to oppose their sieges, thereby persuading other cities to yield without resistance. The dropping of atomic bombs in 1945 had a similar result in forcing the surrender of Japan at the end of World War II. In the heat of battle, the success of terror tactics generally overrides all ethical arguments against their use.

A Japanese painting of 1851 depicts a warrior of the Kusonoki clan advancing undaunted through a storm of arrows. In addition to bearing a tattoo on his face, the soldier wears an elaborate costume and carries a trailing umbrella-like device believed to afford protection from hostile missiles. Masks, sometimes suggesting the faces of monkeys or goblins, were also worn by Japanese soldiers, and among many peoples in Africa and elsewhere, masks were incorporated into flamboyant headdresses—often representing ravens, snakes, or other sacred animals—designed to invoke the aid of supernatural powers. The metal helmets worn by Greek and Roman soldiers—as were those of medieval European knights and other warriors—were designed not just to protect but to terrify an enemy.

The bold, skeleton-like patterns of white pigment adorning the bodies of Aborigine warriors in New South Wales, Australia, as depicted in a painting dated 1813, were intended to frighten enemies and imbue the warriors with a feeling of supernatural power. The practice of fighting naked was itself enough to scare many opponents: A Roman adversary in Britain observed that the Celts "so far despise death that they descend to do battle unclothed." Among other peoples, red (associated with good fortune in war) and black (to bring ill luck to an enemy, and sometimes indicate respect

for the dead) were common colors with which warriors prepared their bodies for battle. Some American Indians were dubbed redskins by white settlers because of the color of their war paint. Scars, indicative of wounds bravely borne, and tattoos were also used to make the human body more terrifying. The word *tattoo* derives from a Polynesian word for the act of striking; it was introduced into English by the eighteenth-century explorer Captain Cook in his description of the Tahitian custom of puncturing the skin and staining the wound in order to leave a permanent mark.

In this nineteenth-century watercolor, Maori warriors off the coast of New Zealand brandish their weapons and bellow a ritual war chant to scare off an approaching ship. A British observer noted that before the Maoris engaged in combat, "they join in a war song to which they all keep the exactest time and, in a short space, raise their passion to a degree of frantic fury attended with the most horrid distortion of their eyes, mouths, and tongues to strike terror in their enemies." Similar battle cries have been widely used: The Roman chronicler of a battle against Celtic warriors in the third century BC recorded that even hardened legionaries were terrified by the effect of "the whole army shouting their war cries at the same time." Bagpipes and other instruments achieved the same purpose: Nineteenth-century Fijian soldiers blew trumpets made from their enemies' bones and beat drums whose skins had been flayed from the same victims. Noise also made weapons more terrifying. The Mongols sometimes pierced their arrows so that they whistled as they flew through the air, while during World War II, some German bombs were fitted with cardboard tubes that caused them to utter a shrieking sound as they descended.

Gripping his reins in his teeth, thereby leaving him free to clutch his booty, a Cossack gallops away from a village he has plundered. The Cossacks, who retained autonomy in the northern hinterlands of the Caspian and Black seas in return for military services to the Russian government, won a reputation for ferocity that is vividly captured in this nineteenth-century French engraving. Other professional warriors who hired themselves out as mercenaries inspired a like dread: Fighting solely for personal gain and unrestrained by any chivalric code, they inflicted atrocities on enemy troops and noncombatants alike. Within standing armies, elite corps whose mere presence has awed an opposing force have included the Ottoman janissaries, Napoleon's Imperial Guard, and the German SS in World War II.

THE AGE OF CHIVALRY

2 "They filled the whole earth with slaughter and panic alike as they flitted hither and thither on their swift horses," wrote the fifth-century scholar Saint Jerome. "They were at hand everywhere before they were expected: By their speed they outstripped rumor, and they took pity neither upon religion nor rank nor age nor wailing childhood." The fast-moving ravagers were the Huns, nomads from central Asia and the latest predators to tear at the half-living carcass of the Roman Empire in the West. The empire's heartbeat in its heyday had been the measured tread of its marching legions; its long downfall was played out against the thunder of hoofs. Even its last defenders had taken to the saddle: When the Huns were turned back at Châlons-sur-Marne in central France in 451, the victors' main strength was in their cavalry. Their commander, the half-Roman, half-Germanic general Aëtius, was noted as a "very practiced horseman"; the men he led had more in common with the Huns they defeated than with the vanished infantry legions to which they were heir.

Fighting on horseback was not a new idea. As early as the ninth century BC, mounted archers had ridden with the conquering armies of Assyria, and horsemen had long dominated warfare in Persia, Arabia, northern China, and parts of India. Even the Romans had deployed cavalry units long before the victory at Châlons. But it was the incursions of the Huns and other mounted marauders from the steppes that shocked Europe into a realization of the cavalry's full potential. Indeed, for almost ten centuries, the principal force in battle, East and West, would be the mounted warrior. Huns, Vandals, Goths, Byzantines, Franks, Normans, Saracens, Mongols—all would fight with armies that depended not on the remorseless discipline of the foot soldier who had won Rome its empire, but on the speed, agility, or sheer mass of the horse.

Ironically, it was in Byzantium, the eastern half of the old empire where the legacy of the legions was strongest, that the best-trained cavalry emerged. The essential role of the Byzantine army was defensive: Although Emperor Justinian I did achieve the temporary reconquest of Italy and North Africa in the sixth century, Byzantium's chief problem was the irresistible temptation that its wealth offered to raiders, who could and did launch attacks from any point on its immensely long frontiers. Since not even the Roman Empire at its zenith had been rich enough to fortify all its borders, Byzantine troops needed to move and concentrate at high speed in order to intercept intruders before they could do any serious damage.

The answer was a professional army in which the cavalry and fast-moving foot archers predominated, with heavy infantry forces usually relegated to garrison and support roles. Armed with bow, broadsword, and lance, the Byzantine horseman was as lethal from a distance as he was close up. The Byzantine historian Procopius, writing in the 550s, observed that the mounted troops were "able without difficulty to direct their bows to either side while riding at full speed and to shoot an opponent

A detail from a fourteenth-century Italian manuscript illustration shows a mounted knight armed with sword, lance, and a shield bearing the heraldic insignia of Robert of Anjou, king of Naples. The use of cavalry in medieval Europe made warfare an increasingly expensive enterprise, and in the mid-thirteenth century, a new technical term—the *lance garnie*—was introduced to denote the combination of equipment and assistants required by a knight while on a campaign. The knight himself rode a light saddle horse when not in battle; his war-horse was led by a mounted squire, who also looked after the packhorse on which the knight's armor was loaded. Two mounted archers completed the team of four men and six horses.

41

This anachronistic depiction of an Old Testament battle includes armor and weapons that were employed during the lifetime of the anonymous French artist in the thirteenth century. The multiform iron helmets and armor of chain mail worn by the horsemen could deflect arrows fired from afar but provided little protection against fierce blows struck at close range. Accordingly, the principal weapons illustrated here—heavy, broad-blade swords, an ax, and a mace—are designed for cleaving rather than for piercing.

whether in pursuit or flight. They draw the bowstring along by the forehead about opposite the right ear, thereby charging an arrow with such impetus as to kill whoever stands in the way, shield and corselet alike having no power to check its force.''

By now, some of the Byzantine cavalry was equipped with the stirrup—a device that reached the Eastern Empire some time in the sixth century. The stirrup is thought to have originated in China in the fourth century and to have been spread westward by the Avars, a steppe tribe that followed the Huns. Its effect was to vastly increase the value of the horse as a fighting platform. Without stirrups, cavalrymen spent much of their effort simply staying in the saddle during combat. But with their feet firmly anchored, they could devote most of their energies to fighting. Broadswords could be swung and lances pressed home with far more vigor than before.

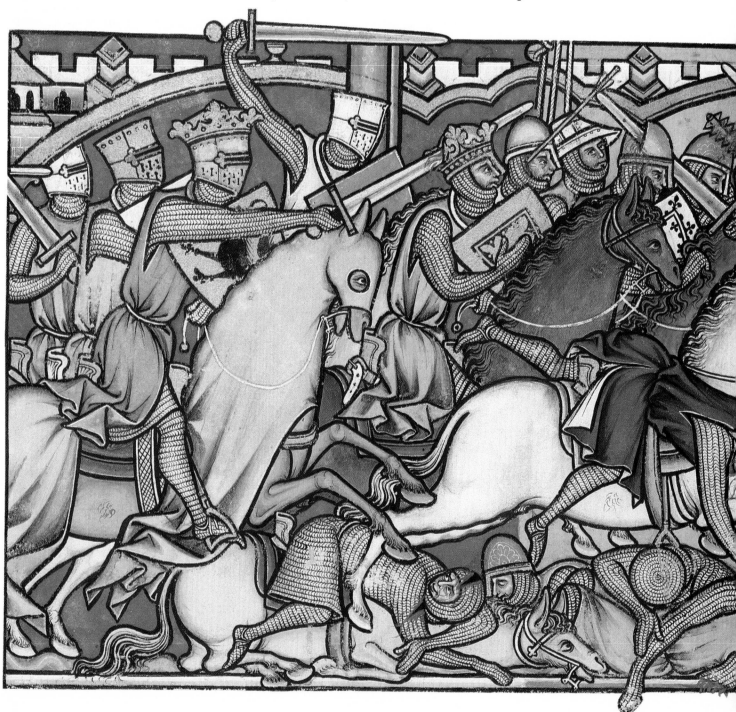

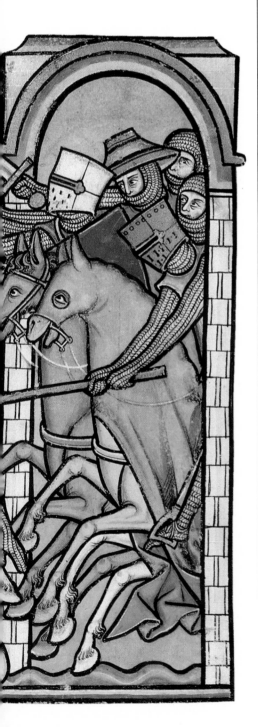

The superiority of the Byzantine military system was dramatically demonstrated during the battle for Rome in 537, when raiding parties of imperial cavalry sallied forth to inflict heavy losses on the besieging Goths. To Procopius, the reason for the victories against the barbarians was clear. "Almost all the Byzantines and their allies, the Avars, are good mounted bowmen," he wrote, "but not a man among the Ostrogoths is practiced in this skill because all their horsemen are accustomed to use only spears and swords. Their archers enter battle on foot and under cover of more heavily armed warriors. Therefore, unless the fighting is at close quarters, the German horsemen cannot defend themselves against mounted archers. As for their foot archers, they can never be strong enough to confront men on horseback."

Against the Gothic charge at Taginae in 552, the eunuch general Narses deployed most of his own heavy cavalry dismounted in defense, with his foot archers placed to bring the advancing enemy under a devastating cross fire. As the Goths retreated in disorder, they were hit by flank attacks from a mounted Byzantine cavalry reserve. Faced with the assault of Frankish infantry units armed with pikes and spears at Casilinum two years later, Narses used the threat of a charge by his cavalry to keep the enemy in a dense, defensive formation that made them an excellent target for Byzantine arrows. As the Franks' formation began to crumble, Narses's horsemen shouldered their bows and charged in to deliver the *coup de grâce* with their lances.

War to the Byzantines was more science than art, certainly an activity far removed from the bloody free-for-all it represented to the barbarians. Their army was always relatively small, in part the consequence of its costly training and equipment, and the limited tax revenues that funded it, but also because of the Byzantine emperors' deep-seated mistrust of the power of their own generals. To compensate for lack of numbers, Byzantine operations were conducted according to a strategy that was expressed in treatises such as the *Strategikon* of about 580, sometimes attributed to the emperor Maurice, and the *Tactica* of Leo VI (the Wise), written around 900.

The empire was divided into military districts—themes—each of which supplied a small but self-contained army corps capable of tackling most situations without outside help. Officers were expected to use whatever combination of arms was appropriate, but were enjoined to caution. Their entire military code was based on winning at minimum cost, which usually meant exploiting their superior discipline, training, and communications to wear down an invading force and drive it from imperial territory without the risk of pitched battle and the loss of expensive troops, who were difficult or impossible to replace. Much time was devoted to studying the strengths and weaknesses of the foe, and there was even an intelligence service, the Office of Barbarians, that passed on valuable information to the field commanders.

The early Byzantine army was remarkable among medieval forces in having a well-organized commissariat and supply system—and with its own logistics reasonably secure, its commanders became adept at turning their enemies' casual or nonexistent supply arrangements against them. Typically, a Byzantine corps encountering a large raiding force would avoid combat, retreating if need be with civilian refugees and livestock to the nearest fortified supply depot. The raiders could either give up and go home, or lay siege to the fort. In either case, the need for food and forage would soon oblige them to disperse, whereupon the theme commander, his own troops concentrated and well fed, would emerge to destroy them piecemeal.

Byzantium's most persistent adversaries, the warriors of Islam, adopted a less-cold-blooded approach to warfare. Inspired by the belief that death in battle would

win them automatic admission to Paradise, they burst out of the Arabian Peninsula with a relentless ferocity that initially swept all before them. Within ten years of the death of the prophet Muhammad in 632, the Muslim armies had not only seized the wealthy imperial provinces of Syria and Egypt but also had swallowed up Byzantium's other mortal enemy, the Persian Empire. The Prophet's soldiers—mostly light cavalry, armed with bow and lance—could match neither the discipline nor the weaponry of their Byzantine opponents. But their new religion imbued them with a soaring morale, their desert origins had given them astonishing powers of endurance, and their light equipment and camel transport made them devastatingly mobile. Furthermore, their small, desert-bred horses, rarely higher than fourteen hands, combined agility, courage, and stamina. The Byzantines and, indeed, other mounted warriors rode only stallions. But the Arabs preferred mares, believing they were more reliable and easier to control than the males of the species.

By the beginning of the eighth century, the tide of Arab conquest had extended westward to the Pyrenees and eastward to Samarkand and the Punjab. After their first encounters with the Byzantines, the Muslim leaders had become increasingly aware of the importance of skill and discipline, and they were quite prepared to adopt the enemy's methods when these seemed superior to their own. As Emperor Leo the Wise noted in his *Tactica:* "Of all the barbarous nations, they are the best advised and the most prudent in their military operations. . . . They have copied the Romans in most of their military practices, both in arms and strategy."

One of the new practices adopted by the Arabs was the use of stirrups. As one Arab chronicler later wrote, these were found to be "among the most useful equipment of war for the spear-wielding lancer and for the swordsman, since both may stand in their stirrups or use them for balance." Another skill learned by these one-time desert dwellers was the besieging of cities. Several times, they tried to capture Constantinople itself. This was an immensely difficult task, since the capital's position—on a narrow promontory surrounded on three sides by water—made it virtually invulnerable to a land attack unsupported by naval forces. By 717, however, the caliph Sulaymān had amassed enough ships to challenge Byzantine control of the Mediterranean and impose an effective blockade. The city was choked with hungry refugees, and although it was protected by massive fortifications, there were barely enough soldiers to defend them. Sulaymān, with an estimated 200,000 men, awaited certain victory. But Byzantium had two unique and devastating weapons.

The first was its emperor, Leo III, a professional soldier who had recently snatched for himself the imperial purple and now proved his fitness for the title. Energetic and aggressive, he twice destroyed a squadron of blockading ships with the second weapon, known as Greek fire—an incendiary liquid of uncertain composition that served as a kind of primitive but highly effective napalm. Squirted from pumps or catapulted in clay pots, it ignited spontaneously even on water, burning scores of ships and terrifying the crews.

Leo followed up his naval attacks with spirited and well-planned sorties from the city against the land-bound besiegers, who suffered even more from a winter passed in trenches at the end of a long and inadequate line of supply. The final blow came in 718, when Leo persuaded the Bulgarians to attack the Arabs from the west. Unable to fight a war on two fronts, they abandoned the siege and returned to their base in Syria. Part of their army marched back through Asia Minor, harassed by Leo's troops. The remainder embarked in Sulaymān's fleet, which was destroyed in a storm. Only 30,000 of the vast force that had set out for Constantinople returned home.

Byzantine defensive skills continued to keep the empire comfortably intact until 1071, when an army led by the emperor Romanus IV clashed with the Seljuk Turks near the Armenian village of Manzikert. Under normal circumstances, Romanus would probably have won. But desertion by his foreign mercenaries and betrayal by one of his own generals led, instead, to a catastrophic defeat. Romanus himself was captured, and thousands of his men were killed or enslaved. While rival claimants struggled for the Byzantine throne, the victorious Seljuks overran the greater part of Asia Minor, the heartland of the empire and the chief recruiting ground of its army. Even so, Islam would not capture Constantinople itself until 1453, and then the victory would depend on a weapon more awesome even than Greek fire.

In the western half of the old Roman Empire, although the barbarian invaders absorbed many aspects of the civilization they had overthrown, they clung to a style of fighting that reflected their own far more diffuse societies. They lived among the descendants of the empire's former citizens, holding land in fealty to a tribal leader, with whom there were often kinship bonds and whose authority they were generally sworn to uphold. But they never trained en masse, and their armies were temporary associations of individuals, not permanent units. In battle, they relied on courage and strength rather than the drilled cohesion that had marked the Roman legions.

There was, however, one among these disorderly and contentious peoples—the Franks—who would establish a system of warfare as pervasive and enduring as that of Rome. On the face of it, they were improbable candidates for such a role. Unlike most of the Germanic tribes that swept through Europe, the Franks had little use for the horse, preferring to wield their traditional swords, spears, and battle-axes while standing firmly on their feet. The impetus for change came from the Muslim Arabs, whose conquest of Spain in 711 brought them within striking distance of the Frankish provinces in France and Germany. The need for mobility against these hard-riding marauders made horsemen essential, and under their war chief Charles Martel—known as the Hammer—the Franks began to make good use of cavalry forces.

In 732, on the bleak plain between Poitiers and Tours, Charles's troops clashed with a Moorish host. Neither army was as large or as sophisticated as the forces engaged at Constantinople fourteen years earlier. The Moors, lightly armored as befitted fast-moving raiders, consisted mainly of swordsmen and lancers: The core of the Hammer's force consisted of his full-time cavalrymen, mailed and helmeted, and armed with spear or battle-ax. Instead of hurling them against the enemy, however, he ordered them to dismount and wait for the Muslims to attack. Though lacking the weight to deliver an effective blow by shock action, the Moors launched charge after futile charge against the spears and shields of Charles's men, who stood, according to a contemporary account, "like a belt of ice frozen together, and not to be dissolved." Eventually, word spread

The use of two simple devices can increase immeasurably a horseman's control over his mount. Stirrups—represented on the opposite page by an early eleventh-century example found in England—bore the rider's full weight as he stood in the saddle to wield lance or spear. Stirrups were introduced to the West around the ninth century from central Asia, where they were used by archers to control their horses as the men charged and drew back their bows. The Bohemian roweled spur shown below is of a type developed in the thirteenth century: Its rotating spikes turned as the horseman pricked his mount, avoiding the injury to the horse often caused by the fixed spike of previous models.

that the leader of the Moors had been killed—news that so disheartened his men that they promptly fled back to Spain. Although the Muslim threat to western Europe would not be extinguished for another two decades, the worst crisis had passed.

Charles's decision to use his horsemen as foot soldiers was based on a realistic assessment of their limitations. Not only were they much slower than the Muslims, they were also reckless, obstinate, and unruly. The Byzantine emperor Leo the Wise summed up the reputation of the Frankish cavalry well: He acknowleged their daring and courage, but observed that they had "neither organization nor discipline. . . . Hence, they readily fall into confusion if suddenly attacked in flank and rear—a thing easy to accomplish, as they are utterly careless and neglect the use of outposts and reconnaissance. Nothing succeeds better against them than a feigned flight that draws them into an ambush; for they follow hastily and invariably fall into the snare."

If the new class of mounted warriors, with their expensive armor, weapons, and horses, was to be maintained, society had to change. In eighth-century France and Germany, such costs could be met only by granting lands to the cavalrymen in return for their service. From the 730s on, Charles and his heirs seized vast estates from the Church and redistributed them to their nobles, who in return, were obliged to contribute mounted soldiers to the royal army in time of war. The nobles obtained the services of these professional cavalrymen by investing them with their own tracts of land, or fiefs, whose revenues enabled them to buy their steeds and equipment. Thus, the warrior was the vassal of his lord, as was the lord of his superior, the king.

The Church, itself a major beneficiary of the security that could be provided by the mounted men it had unwillingly paid for, was forgiving: It conferred on Charles's grandson, Charles the Great—Charlemagne—the imperial title. The West now had an emperor to rival those of the East. A dynamic and daring war leader, Charlemagne was the epitome of the warrior-hero. A vivid picture of the emperor was provided by a chronicler in the 870s: "Then appeared the iron king, crowned with his iron helm, with sleeves of iron mail and his breast protected by a mail shirt, an iron lance in his left hand, his right hand free to carry his unconquered sword."

The Frankish empire reached its zenith under Charlemagne, who extended its borders from the Ebro to the Elbe rivers. Throughout this vast area, the system of mounted men supported by landholdings was extended and consolidated. And although the empire itself disappeared in all but name with the death of Charlemagne in 814, its military structure survived, which was just as well. For the next century and a half, the Frankish lands were assailed by incessant waves of invaders—the Vikings from the north, the Avars and Magyars from the east, and the Muslims from the south. It was in the struggle against these predators that the new class of feudal horse-warriors, or knights, achieved complete military and social preeminence.

Only the Anglo-Saxons, isolated in their island backwater of England, continued to fight on foot—a tactic that cost them dearly when faced with the Norman invasion of 1066. The Normans were descendants of Viking raiders who had settled in northern France, and it may have been their Norse blood that had made them such formidable soldiers. As one chronicler described them, "They are a race inured to war and can hardly live without it, fierce in rushing against the enemy and, when strength fails of success, ready to use stratagem or to corrupt by bribery. . . . They are faithful to their lords, although slight offense renders them perfidious."

William II of Normandy was a leader with a profound sense of his own authority and extensive warfare experience. "It was a sight both delightful and terrible," wrote one observer, "to see him managing his horse, girt with sword, his shield gleaming, his helmet and his lance alike gleaming. For as he looked magnificent in princely apparel or the habiliments of peace, so to be in his war gear especially became him."

In the summer of 1066, with a plausible claim to the throne of a troubled England, William crossed the Channel with a substantial force to confront the army of King Harold II. This army was made up of the royal guard, well-trained and highly disciplined, and a rough-and-ready peasant militia levied for the occasion. The royal guard members were heavily armed, the peasants indifferently; but all fought on foot with spear, ax, and sword—they had few bowmen—behind the kind of shield wall that Charles Martel would have recognized. Harold's army was both tough and courageous, but it was completely outclassed by William's new-style force, in which mailed cavalrymen were supported by archers and well-armed heavy infantry units.

The decisive action came soon after the Norman landing. Harold, spurning advice to delay until more of his nobles might gather, had marched briskly south from London—most of his elite troops had horses for transport—and entrenched himself on a hillside near Hastings that dominated the main road from the coast to the capital, and whose steep slopes protected his flanks. But once he had planted his banner on the summit, Harold could only await the invaders' assault. He was well aware that, once his men broke ranks, they would be at the mercy of the Norman cavalry.

Eager to meet his opponents, William advanced toward their position and opened the contest early on the morning of October 14. The first to go into action were the Norman archers, some armed with the shortbow and some with the crossbow. Though known in classical times, the crossbow had vanished with the Roman legions, and Hastings marked its first recorded appearance on a European battlefield in almost 500 years. After his archers' opening volley, most of which was deflected by

In an illustration taken from a 1573 edition of an Italian manual devoted to horsemanship, three men begin breaking in a horse before training it to the standards of obedience and agility that were required in warfare. A well-trained war-horse was worth several hundred times as much as a peasant's workhorse. For much of the medieval period, strength and size were the most important attributes of horses bred for battle, but during the sixteenth century, lighter, more maneuverable mounts found favor, first in the courts of Renaissance Italy and then across the rest of Europe.

the English shield wall, William sent his infantry up the hill to probe the enemy line. They were driven off. Next, he launched a massive cavalry assault. According to one story, a Norman minstrel named Taillefer spurred his horse forward in front of his advancing comrades and regaled them with a song about the exploits of two earlier heroes—the emperor Charlemagne and Charlemagne's nephew, Roland. Alone, Taillefer rushed at the English line, killing several of the enemy before he was himself struck down. The knights who followed made equally little impression on the English, some of whom wielded huge battle-axes that could decapitate a horse.

As the knights fell back, some of the less-disciplined English broke ranks to pursue. They were at once ridden down by fresh Norman cavalrymen, led by William himself. Another attack and another retreat had the same effect. As the chronicler William of Poitiers later described it: "The barbarians exulted with the hope of victory. Exhorting each other with triumphant shouts, they poured scorn upon our men and boasted that they would all be destroyed then and there. As before, some thousands of them were bold enough to launch themselves as if on wings after those they thought to be fleeing. The Normans, suddenly wheeling their horses about, cut them off, surrounded them, and slew them on all sides, leaving not one alive."

But the shield wall continued to hold, and even the wildest of the English troops now realized that a counterattack in the face of William's terrible horsemen meant certain death. The duke changed his tactics. His archers lashed the hill with arrows, shooting high in the air so that their missiles fell on the massed ranks behind the shield wall. Arrow showers alternated with more cavalry attacks on the increasingly exhausted defenders, who could do nothing to relieve their torment. In the memorable words of one chronicler, "in the English ranks, the only movement was the dropping of the dead: The living stood motionless." At last, just after twilight, King Harold was hit in the eye by an arrow, and his followers, their morale crushed, broke and fled, pursued by the Norman cavalry. A month later, William entered London and on Christmas Day, 1066, was crowned king of the English.

The Bayeux tapestry suggests that William's cavalry used their lances for both throwing and stabbing. Sometime during the later eleventh century, they began to use a technique that was much more devastating. With his lance couched—holding the stock tightly under the armpit and directing the point straight ahead—and seated in a saddle with a raised and reinforced back, which prevented him from being thrust off his horse on the shock of impact, the charging knight became an almost unstoppable projectile. According to the daughter of Byzantine emperor Alexius I Comnenus, "a Frank with a lance in his hand could punch a hole in the walls of Babylon."

Brought up from early boyhood in the practice of arms, the knight was bound by the code of chivalry. The word *chivalry* derived from the Old French *chevalerie*,

meaning horsemanship, and from this also came *cavalry* and *cavalier*. The chivalric code blended Christian ideals with Germanic concepts of honor and loyalty and provided the standards by which the good knight was supposed to live. "What is the function of orderly knighthood?" wrote the twelfth-century English philosopher John of Salisbury. "To protect the Church, to fight against treachery, to reverence the priesthood, to fend off injustice from the poor, to make peace in your own province, to shed blood for your brethren, and if need be, to lay down your life."

The training of an aspiring knight conventionally began in his seventh year, when he was sent to the court of a nobleman connected with his family. Here, away from the distracting influence of his mother, he would spend several years as a page, waiting on the lord and his lady at table, learning the social graces—including singing, dancing, and lute playing—and receiving basic lessons in weaponry and horsemanship. At the age of fourteen, the page became a knight's squire, with the duty of attending his master both in the hall and on the field. He cared for his knight's weapons and horses, helped him buckle on his armor, and tended his wounds. He also completed his own military education. He would take part in games and mock battles and test his equestrian skills by riding full tilt at the quintain. The last was an upright post with a pivoted crossbar at the top. On one end of the bar was a target, and from the other was suspended a bag of sand that would swing around and hit a charging horseman in the back unless he was fast enough to get out of the way.

At the age of twenty-one, with the approval of his master, the novice was formally admitted to knighthood. At first, this was an entirely secular affair, but by 1200, it had become a largely religious occasion. On the eve of the ceremony, the candidate took a symbolic bath, donned a clean white robe and a red mantle, and remained in a nightlong vigil before the altar on which his weapons and armor lay. At dawn, Mass was performed before an audience of friends, family, nobles, and knights. The initiate then received his sword, belt, and spurs, each blessed and consecrated to the service of heaven. The spurs were usually put on first and came to be regarded as the chief symbol of knighthood. If found guilty of cowardice or any other dishonorable act, a knight had his spurs hacked off as a sign of his humiliation.

The candidate, having taken the vows of knighthood—for example, to defend the Church, to succor the poor and oppressed, to pursue evildoers, never to retreat before an enemy—then received the accolade. This was a symbolic blow on the neck or cheek from either the hand or the flat of a sword and was normally delivered by a knight of renown. According to one thirteenth-century account, the blow symbolized the awakening of the initiate into the new life of knighthood.

"Gentle knights were born to fight," wrote the fourteenth-century French chronicler Jean Froissart, "and war ennobles all who engage in it without fear or coward-

A section from the eleventh-century Bayeux tapestry shows soldiers and horses of the Norman army of William the Conqueror disembarking on the southeast coast of England in 1066. The invasion fleet of flat-bottomed boats—which could be easily beached—carried some 7,000 men and 3,000 cavalry mounts. The Normans acquired horses of African stock from Spain and Arabian horses from Sicily, and these stallions, specially bred for warfare, brought them victory in the battle against the English army at Hastings.

A detail from a sixteenth-century Japanese screen shows a swordsmith sharpening a blade on a whetstone while his companion burnishes a finished article. A woman attempts to attract their attention from outside the door: Only the smith's assistant was allowed to enter the workshop, and the smith himself abjured meat, alcohol, and sex during the time of forging.

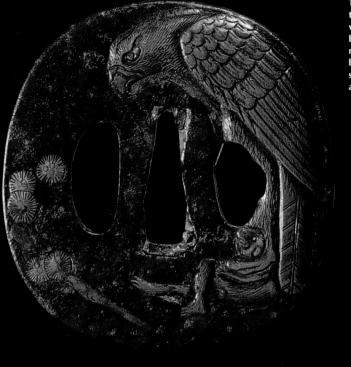

The central hole pierced in this iron sword guard—which is engraved with a brass eagle clutching a monkey—admits the main blade. On either side of it, shorter blades might be attached as well.

Forged in the early fourteenth century by Masamune, one of the finest Japanese swordsmiths, this sword has the characteristic shallow curve of blades designed for sweeping cuts rather than for thrusting.

SAMURAI STEEL

No mere tool or implement, the sword of a Japanese samurai warrior was invested with a spiritual significance appropriate to the high social status of its wearer. Unsheathing his weapon, the warrior took part in a ritual code of honor of which the sword was the very soul.

The swordsmiths who made these weapons were the highest-ranking artisans, with reputations akin to the jewelers in Europe. Formed from different grades of steel or sometimes from steel and iron combined, the sword was forged in a fire of pine-charcoal and was welded, hammered, and re-formed as many as twenty times. The blade was tempered over fire to give it a cutting edge that could be ground to a razorlike sharpness and was then polished and sometimes inscribed with the name of the smith. It was secured to a wooden hilt with a collar, guard, and pegs that were made of horn or bamboo.

Each samurai sword was said to take on the character traits of its maker. According to a traditional Japanese story, the swords of two rival smiths were once put to a test in a gently flowing stream: The floating leaves that met one blade were cut cleanly in two, while those nearing the other blade moved aside to avoid it—thus proving the ferocity of the first swordmaker and the essential nobility of the second.

ice." In lieu of a war, the knight could seek fame and fortune by competing in tournaments. These supposedly mock battles hardly differed from the real thing and often resulted in numerous casualties and deaths. William Marshal, a famous champion of the twelfth century who later became regent of England, once received such a severe blow to the head that a blacksmith had to remove his helmet. At a tournament held in 1241 at Neuss in Germany, some eighty knights and squires were killed. As one chronicler put it: "A knight cannot shine in war if he has not prepared for it in tournaments. He must have seen his own blood flow, have been dashed to the earth with such force as to feel the weight of his foe, and have been disarmed twenty times; he must twenty times have retrieved his failures, more set than ever upon the combat. Then he will be able to confront actual war with hope of being victorious."

Even after the introduction of rules designed to make the sport safer—insisting on the use of blunted weapons, for example, and restricting the number of retainers who could be armed—fatalities still occurred. In 1130, the Church imposed a ban on tournaments, decreeing that those killed in such contests would be denied a Christian burial. From time to time, secular rulers also tried to suppress these martial contests, but they continued to exert an irresistible lure for participants and onlookers alike.

The knightly ethos was celebrated by warrior-poets, or troubadours, such as Bertran de Born—a favorite of Eleanor of Aquitaine, queen first of Louis VII of France and then of Henry II of England—who wrote of how he loved to "see a lord when he is first to advance on horseback, armed and fearless, thus encouraging his men to valiant service: Then, when the fray has begun, each must be ready to follow him willingly, because no one is held in esteem until he has given and received blows. . . . Once he has started fighting, no noble knight thinks of anything but breaking heads and arms—better a dead man than a live one who is useless. . . . Barons, you should rather forfeit castles, towns, and cities than give up—any of you—going to war."

"Going to war" in medieval Europe rarely meant going into battle, for battles were few, and decisive battles such as Hastings occurred hardly at all. The trouble was that mass combat was risky and unpredictable. A leader could plan his campaign to bring his men into the field against the enemy in the most advantageous position, but once they were committed to action, there was very little he could do to control events—especially as he was usually in the thick of the fray himself, where his followers expected him to be. In an address to his army before its defeat by the English at the Battle of Falkirk in 1298, the Scottish war leader William Wallace neatly summed up the situation: "I have brought you to the ring; now hop if you can."

Commanders usually avoided such confrontations, preferring instead to mount *chevauchées*—or mounted raids—on the territories of their opponents. Parties of armed horsemen would descend on a village, burn the buildings, and seize or destroy the crops and livestock. In such situations, the knightly vow to help the poor and oppressed would be conveniently forgotten, and any inhabitants who tried to resist would be mercilessly killed. "When two nobles quarrel," wrote a contemporary, "the poor man's thatch goes up in flames."

In the unlikely event that a pitched battle did occur, the number of casualties—at least among the cavalry—was usually very small. In 1119, at Bremule in Normandy, for example, Henry I of England and 500 knights intercepted a foray led by Louis VI of France and about 400 men. The French were soundly defeated, but a long afternoon's work with sword and lance resulted in only three fatalities. As one chronicler smugly observed, they "spared each other on both sides out of fear of God and fellowship in arms; they were more concerned to capture than to kill the fugitives." Chivalry was certainly a restraining influence in such clashes, but so, too, was the knowledge that an enemy knight was more valuable alive than dead. Captives could usually fetch a handsome sum in ransom from relatives or feudal lords.

For the most part, knight fought knight, but sometimes a clash between knights and foot soldiers was unavoidable. These were conflicts to which the code of chivalry did not apply, and the infantry, consisting mainly of conscripted peasants, was regarded as eminently expendable. So great was the contempt of the French cavalry for foot soldiers that they were liable to ride down their own infantrymen if they got in the way. This attitude was fully reciprocated. Although foot soldiers might spare a fallen knight in the hope of a share in his ransom, they were just as likely to hammer an iron spike through the chinks in his armor as he lay helpless on the ground.

The Church played a major part in defining what was and what was not acceptable in warfare. In the fifth century, Saint Augustine had preached the doctrine of the "just" war—in essence, the struggle by a lawful power or authority to resist injury by an enemy. Clerics themselves were not averse to fighting in what they regarded as a righteous cause. Froissart recorded that at the Battle of Otterburn in 1388, the chaplain to the Earl of Douglas "struck out and helped to drive back the English by ax blows, which he rained and beat down fiercely on them."

In the late tenth century, the Church began to preach a so-called Peace of God that gave immunity to noncombatants. This was followed in the early eleventh century by the Truce of God, which imposed a ban on all fighting from 9:00 p.m. on Saturday to daybreak on Monday. The Church also tried to restrict the use of missile weapons—notably the crossbow, which had come into widespread use in the West, particularly among mercenary soldiers. Much more powerful than the handbow, it was capable of knocking a rider from his saddle at more than 300 feet and could be fired accurately with little training. In 1096, it was condemned by Pope Urban II as "hateful to God," and in 1139, it was duly banned by the Second Lateran Council.

No such scruples intruded into the warfare waged against pagans. Indeed, the Church believed that an effective way of reducing violence between Christians was to direct it against non-Christians, and there were no better candidates than the

In this early fourteenth-century manuscript illustration, Louis IX of France, blessed by a host of monks, embarks on the Sixth Crusade in 1248 to liberate the Christian holy places from Muslim rule. The campaign was a military disaster: His army was stricken with plague and defeated in Egypt, and Louis himself was captured. Freed for a high ransom, he led another Crusade in 1270 but died in Tunisia. The depth of Louis's piety—he wore a hair shirt, fasted regularly, and kept constant company with priests and monks—was matched by his martial fervor: Any layman hearing the Christian religion abused, he said, "should not attempt to defend its tenets except with the sword, and that he should thrust into the scoundrel's belly as far as it will enter."

TURKEY

Sis

Ilan • Tilium

Selef • Corycus

Anamur •

Gastun

Antioch•

Edessa •

Orontes River

Euphrates River

Saint Hilarion • • Kyrenia

Saone • Apamea

CYPRUS

Margat

Famagusta

Tortosa • Castel Blanc

Chastel Rouge • Krak des Chevaliers

Arima • Akkar

Kolossi •

Tripoli

SYRIAN DESERT

Gibelet

Mediterranean Sea

Litani River

Tyron •

Beaufort •

Acre • Paneas

Chastel Pelerin • Montfort

Sea of Galilee

Belvoir •

Jordan River

Jerusalem•

Dead Sea

• Krak de Montreal

Muslim pagans who occupied the Holy Land. As Pope Urban II proclaimed: "Let those who formerly contended against their brothers now fight as they ought, against the barbarians." In many ways, the First Crusade, preached by Urban in 1095, was one of history's most improbable adventures. A few thousand knights from every part of the Continent—to Muslims, every infidel invader from the West was a "Frank"—a generous supply of ill-organized infantry forces, and a mass of hopeful pilgrims set off for Palestine in 1097. Once they arrived, those who survived the journey captured Jerusalem from an Islamic world whose military resources, at least in theory, were vastly superior, and held at least some of their gains for two centuries before a shamed and affronted Islam finally expelled the last of them. There were many reasons for the delay, of which Muslim disunity remains the most convincing. But in the eyes of Western Christendom, there was one obvious explanation: the armored knight.

As every Crusader, from the loftiest prince to the lowliest pilgrim, was well aware, the army's great strength lay in its heavy cavalry. Given a fixed objective and enough space to accelerate to a lumbering gallop, the knights were irresistible. But the knights could be relied on for only one massed charge; it was almost impossible to recall and reform them for another. Crusader commanders had to judge the timing of the charge perfectly—and keep their impetuous horsemen in order until the right moment.

If their first tactical problem was set by the nature of their own army, the second was provided by the nature of their enemy—the Saracens, as the Crusaders called them, a name that served to describe Arab and Turk alike. Their main opponents were, in fact, Seljuk Turks, who relied on cavalry of a very different kind: lightly armored horse-archers, who launched wave upon wave of arrows and closed in with lance and sword only after their arrows had inflicted heavy losses on the enemy. They were faster and more agile than any knight, and unless they could be pinned against an obstacle—a river, for instance, or a judiciously placed Crusader detachment—a charge had no more effect on them than a sword slicing through a cloud of gnats.

But perhaps the greatest enemy of the Western soldiers was the climate. Marching and fighting in burning heat, they were plagued by illness, thirst, and exhaustion. Their problem was made worse by the Turks' practice of poisoning the wells. Raymond of Aguilers, chaplain to the Count of Toulouse, recorded how the Crusaders fought one another to drink at the pool of Siloam, near Jerusalem. "Those who were strong enough pushed and shoved their way in a deathly fashion through the pool, which was already choked with dead animals and men struggling for their lives . . . those who were weaker sprawled on the ground beside the pool with gaping mouths, their parched tongues making them speechless, while they stretched out their hands to beg water from the more fortunate ones. In the nearby fields, horses, mules, cattle, sheep, and many other animals were standing too weak to move. They shriveled and died of thirst, rotting where they stood, and filled the air with the smell of death."

The Turks had tactical problems of their own. Although their arrows could kill and wound horses and the less-well-equipped Crusader infantry, they lacked the power to penetrate the heavy armor of the Crusader cavalry. Even in close combat, their weapons were frequently ineffective against Frankish mail and helm. Furthermore, the Crusaders excelled in siege warfare, and within a few months, they had captured Edessa, Antioch, and several other towns. On one occasion, following a promise that their lives would be spared, the inhabitants surrendered: Once they had gained access to the town, however, the Crusaders began a massacre that went on for three days. But as the Frankish chronicler Radulph of Caen later confessed, the invaders

The map on the left shows the locations of the principal castles built by the European Crusaders in the twelfth century to secure and defend the territory they had conquered in the Holy Land. Rarely more than 50 miles inland from a 185-mile-long coastline, the castles enabled the Christians to withstand the onslaughts of vastly more numerous Muslim forces for two centuries; they were garrisoned by members of Christian military orders originally founded to protect pilgrims visiting holy sites. Inset is a photograph of the Krak des Chevaliers, built about 2,300 feet above sea level to command a strategic valley: Defended by two rings of walls and a wide moat, this castle was described by an Arab historian as a "bone in the throat of the Muslims."

THE SIEGE MENTALITY

In medieval warfare, sieges were not only more common than pitched battles but also a more severe test of the contestants' endurance and ingenuity. Defenders relied on stone or brick walls, moats, and dry ditches; attackers used diverse tactics and contraptions designed both to breach defenses and to minimize their own casualties.

Walls could often be undermined: A tunnel was dug and supported with timber props, then a fire was set to collapse both the tunnel and the wall above it. Wooden siege towers draped with wet hides to pro-tect them from burning sheltered the attackers as they approached a wall; while those at the top of the tower fought hand-to-hand with defenders, their fellow soldiers below pounded the wall with a battering ram. And a variety of siege engines—many of them resembling giant catapults or crossbows—were devised to hurl projectiles against or over a defensive wall. The machines of the Arabs, whose technology and science far excelled those of the West, incorporated gears and winches and were noted for their range and accuracy.

In this fourteenth-century Persian manuscript painting, central Asian besiegers use a massive catapult to assault a fortress. A turbaned Arab supervises the loading of the sling with round stones: When released, the counterweight at the front of the machine sent the balls hurtling toward the enemy.

were not content simply to kill. They also "boiled pagan adults in cooking pots" and "impaled children on spits and devoured them grilled."

In July 1099, after a brief siege, the Crusaders captured Jerusalem itself. It was an astonishing feat of arms, though brutally marred by the ensuing slaughter of most of the Holy City's surviving population, Muslim, Jew, and Christian alike—again, even the Crusaders' own chroniclers felt their behavior had been shameful.

The states their leaders went on to found—Jerusalem, Antioch, Edessa, and Tripoli—though under constant Muslim attack, generally managed to hold their own until the 1190s. Of the innumerable campaigns fought in Syria and Palestine during the twelfth century, however, very few involved pitched battles. Full-scale fighting was avoided for the same reasons as in Europe, with additional restraint imposed on the Crusaders because of their limited numbers and their distance from reinforcements. As a result, the Crusaders became adroit castle builders, and most campaigns had as their object the capture and defense of strongpoints.

The greatest risk for the Crusaders was to be caught in the open by their opponents. Typically, they would find themselves surrounded by Turkish horse-archers, capable of keeping up a harassing attack on a marching column. If the Crusaders succeeded in maintaining a close-ranked formation, the Turkish arrows were more galling than dangerous, although they regularly killed or wounded the unarmored. Often, however, a group of infuriated knights would abandon march discipline and charge at their tormentors, in which case the knights would usually disappear forever amid a flurry of Turkish horsemen. These running fights could continue for days. The Crusader forces, carrying their dead and wounded, could only plod onward through the enervating heat, which was often compounded by smoke from heathland fired by the enemy. But the Turks also suffered in this kind of combat, since the Crusader crossbows usually did more harm than the light bows of their own horsemen. Although the Crusader cavalry refused to use missile weapons, considering them at odds with the knightly ethos of individual combat, they had no objection to their use by the infantry.

As a Turkish participant in one such skirmish sourly wrote: "Each foot soldier wore a thick cassock of felt and under it a mail shirt so strong that our arrows made no impression on them. They, meanwhile, shot at us with crossbows, which struck down horse and man among the Muslims. I noted among them men who had from one to ten shafts sticking in their backs, yet trudged on at their ordinary pace and did not fall out of their ranks. . . . The Franks continued to advance in this order, fighting vigorously all the way. The Muslims sent in volleys of arrows from all sides, endeavoring to irritate the knights into leaving their ramparts of infantry. But it was all in vain. . . . It was impossible not to admire the patience these people showed."

Sometimes, the ceaseless Turkish attacks brought glorious results. In 1187, the entire Crusader field army, on a fifteen-mile march through waterless desert to relieve the Galilee town of Tiberias from a Muslim siege, was forced to halt in arid country far short of its destination, its rearguard infantry fatally separated from the knights. The next morning, on the Horns of Hattin, the exhausted, thirst-racked Crusaders were killed or captured almost to a man. After Hattin, a demoralized Jerusalem surrendered after only twelve days' siege, and thenceforth the Crusaders were relegated to a long coastal strip, which they held only because of the supporting sea power of Venice and Genoa. Although the embers of the remnant Crusader states glowed a little longer and there were still a few Frankish victories to come, by the end of the thirteenth century, the main Western outposts had been extinguished.

Meanwhile, Muslims and Christians had been contending with an enemy more terrible than either of them—the Mongols. A fierce nomadic people from the steppes of central Asia, they burst on the world in 1211, led by a chief whose total authority earned him the title Genghis Khan—or Universal King. The Mongols were immensely skilled horsemen—their lives, as herdsmen and hunters, depended on their mounts—and their army was divided mainly into horse-archers (equipped with powerful compound bows and able to hit a moving target at almost 1,000 feet) and lancers. Other steppe peoples, similarly arrayed, had been difficult to counter. But the Mongols were a greater menace still, for under Genghis Khan, they added discipline to the traditional nomadic strengths of stamina and mobility.

"Their horses are fed upon grass alone," observed the Venetian traveler Marco Polo, "and do not require barley or other grain. The men are habituated to remain on horseback during two days and two nights, without dismounting; sleeping in that situation while their horses graze. . . . Their horses are so well broken in to quick changes of movement that, upon the signal given, they instantly turn in every direction; and by these rapid movements, many victories have been obtained."

Their army, 150,000 strong and including every Mongol male between the ages of sixteen and sixty, was organized on a decimal system of units: A troop comprised 10 men, a squadron 10 troops, a regiment 10 squadrons. The principal fighting formation was the division, or *tümen,* of 10 regiments—10,000 men. Because the Mongols rigorously obeyed orders, the commanders of these subunits enjoyed a large measure of tactical control, the more so since Mongol leaders did not plunge into the thick of a fight but invariably stayed back with their reserves to direct the battle. To match their field discipline, Mongol commanders had something akin to a general staff to help them, as well as a commissariat of Byzantine efficiency. The result, at least for a time, was an empire that extended from the Pacific Ocean to the Mediterranean.

The Jin empire was the first to fall, providing the great khan with a vast new territory, as well as a train of Chinese siege engineers. Before the Chinese campaign was concluded, he turned his attention westward, conquering the powerful Islamic state of Khwarizm, successor to ancient Persia. But its inhabitants rebelled against their new masters, killing some of the thinly spread Mongol garrisons. The great khan reacted savagely. A huge Mongol army swept through the territory of Transoxiana, looting, burning, and killing. So great was the devastation that the contemporary Arab historian Ibn al-Athīr was moved to describe it as "a tremendous disaster such as has never happened before. It may well be that the world from now until its end will not experience the like of it again, apart perhaps from Gog and Magog."

With the death of Genghis Khan in 1227, supreme authority passed to his third son, Ogedei. A grandson, Batu Khan, was entrusted with the conquest of Russia and Europe. Since the rivers and marshes of central Russia were a bar to the rapid movement on which the Mongols depended, Batu attacked in midwinter, when these obstacles were frozen. For any other army, it would have been a disastrous folly. But thanks to Mongol discipline and the superb Mongol commissariat, the whirlwind campaign of 1237 and 1238 was a triumphant success—though a catastrophe for the northern Russian principalities that succumbed to it. The Ukrainian city of Kiev fell in 1240; that same year, the Mongols pushed westward into Poland and Hungary.

Nothing, it seemed, could stand against them. In April 1241, at Liegnitz, the armored cavalry of Germany and Poland was annihilated by the rapid and coordinated movements of an army that responded to its commander as a horse to a rider.

Two days later, Hungary's king Béla IV and his knights met the same fate at the Sajó River. While the main Mongol force relaxed on the Hungarian plain, advance guards probed as far west as Wiener Neustadt, almost at the gates of Vienna.

There was no reason to believe that the knights of France or England could put up a better resistance. Besides, western Europe was in more than usual disarray, with emperor and pope engaged in a vicious quarrel. But if Batu and his staff had any plans for further conquest, they were never put into effect. In December 1241, Ogedei died in central Asia. When Batu moved, he moved east, to protect his claims to the great khan's inheritance. Europe was given a welcome reprieve.

The Mongol conquests represented the high-water mark of cavalry warfare. The balance would now tilt steadily back in the direction of the foot soldier. The change began to become apparent in western Europe early in the fourteenth century, when the crossbow was overshadowed by an even more lethal missile weapon—the English longbow. Originally used by the Welsh, it became a crucial weapon of the English forces in the Hundred Years' War against France. The longbow not only had more than twice the range of the crossbow—up to 750 feet —but also a far more rapid rate of fire. In the hands of a skilled archer, it could fire twelve arrows a minute.

At the Battle of Crécy in 1346, the French armored cavalry charged again and again toward the English lines, only to be brought down by a hail of arrows. "For the bowmen," wrote Jean Froissart, "let fly among them at large, and did not lose a single shaft, for every arrow told on horse or man, piercing head, or arm, or leg among the riders and sending the horses mad." Taking advantage of the confusion, Welsh and Irish foot soldiers armed with daggers rushed from the English ranks and "falling upon earls, barons, knights, and squires, slew many, at which the king of England was afterward much exasperated." The king, no doubt, had been looking forward to a rich harvest of ransoms. After fifteen futile assaults, the battered French withdrew, leaving, by one count, 1,542 lords and knights and some 10,000 other ranks dead on the field. The English, for their part, lost only 200 dead, including two knights.

The French cavalry's response to Crécy was to provide themselves with better protection, and by the mid-fourteenth century, they were abandoning chain mail for plate armor—an initiative that was followed throughout western Europe. Although a casing of polished steel was an effective defense against more missiles, it reduced mobility—and mobility was the essential characteristic of the mounted warrior. Burdened with some 110 pounds of armor and equipment, a cavalry horse could manage little more than a slow trot. When the armored knight dismounted, he was severely hampered by heat and lack of ventilation and found it easy to fight only in a stationary position. In 1415, at the Battle of Agincourt, mounted French knights advancing on the English lines were easily outflanked by the enemy archers, who then let loose with devastating fire at short range. Struggling and slithering on the muddy ground, many of the French were drowned or trampled to death by their own comrades. Others were dispatched by the English archers wielding knives and clubs. By the end of the day, the French had lost some 5,000 men, the English a few hundred.

Advancing technology would tilt the military balance still further. Few of the struggling French even noticed the curious little "firepots" discharged at them by a handful of adventurous Englishmen at Crécy. Within a century, though, gunpowder weapons would have begun to transform the battlefield. The infantryman would quickly adapt. But the armored knight, once the terror and the pride of Europe, would become as extinct as Caesar's legions.

THE IRONCLAD KNIGHT

The irresistible force that was the mounted European knight at a full gallop was as much a product of military engineering as were the fortress and siege gun. At the beginning of the Middle Ages, warriors were protected at best by an iron helmet and a shirt of mail, constructed of interlinked iron rings; by the early 1400s, however, many knights were clanking into battle encased in as many as 200 separate pieces of plate armor that could deflect swords, spears, arrows, and crossbow bolts.

Articulated joints in this armor allowed for considerable maneuverability—a fully clad knight, for example, was well able to mount his horse unaided—and by the sixteenth century, many suits of armor included interchangeable sections appropriate for battle or tournament, and for fighting on foot or on horseback. At the very time that the design of armor was nearing perfection, however, combat was being transformed by cannon and muskets—whose explosive power would rapidly turn the armored knight into an antique curiosity.

A composite suit of armor for man and horse made of low-carbon steel in Germany in the late fifteenth century exhibits the spiky elegance of the Gothic style. Grooves and ridges were both decorative and functional, being designed to deflect arrows from vital body parts.

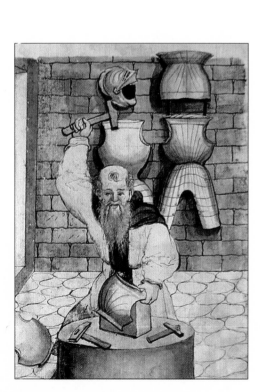

An armorer hammers a breastplate into shape in a sixteenth-century workshop in the city of Nuremberg, located at the heart of an iron-producing region and one of the main centers of armor manufacture in Europe.

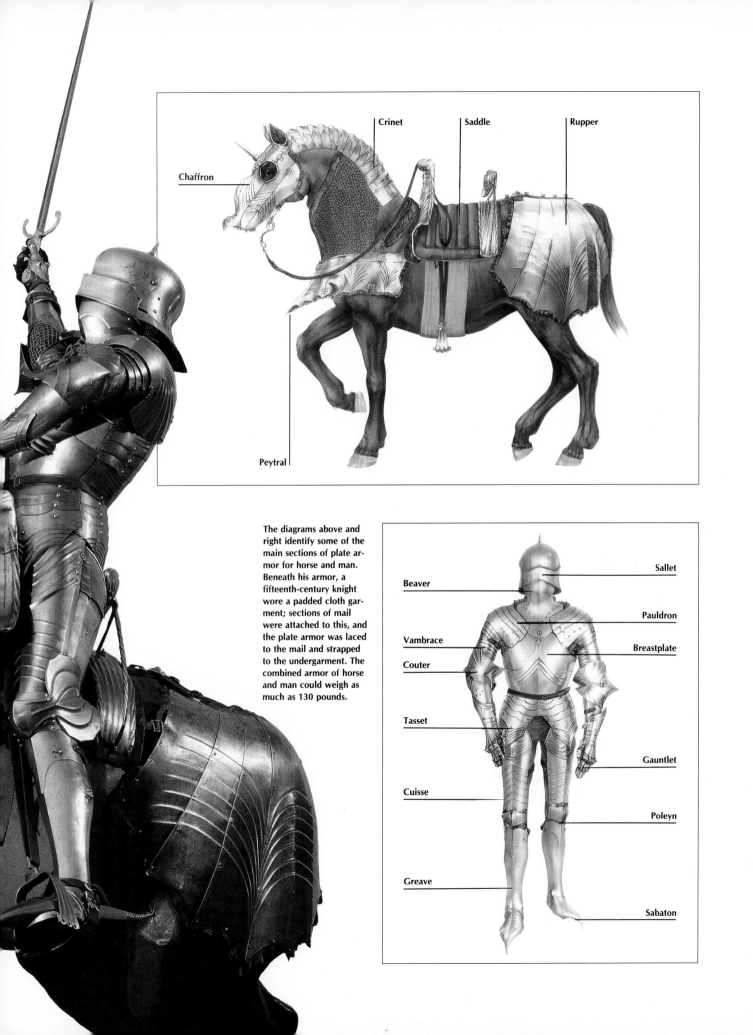

Chaffron

Crinet

Saddle

Rupper

Peytral

The diagrams above and right identify some of the main sections of plate armor for horse and man. Beneath his armor, a fifteenth-century knight wore a padded cloth garment; sections of mail were attached to this, and the plate armor was laced to the mail and strapped to the undergarment. The combined armor of horse and man could weigh as much as 130 pounds.

Beaver

Vambrace

Couter

Tasset

Cuisse

Greave

Sallet

Pauldron

Breastplate

Gauntlet

Poleyn

Sabaton

A NEW KIND OF WAR

King Charles VIII of France was in a triumphant mood. A few months earlier, in September 1494, he had led an army of 18,000 across the Alps into Italy to make good his claim to the throne of Naples. Equipped with a horse-drawn siege train of about forty cannon, the invaders had swept aside all opposition, and by February 4, 1495, they had reached the towering fortress of Monte San Giovanni, only a few miles from the city of Naples itself. The fortress had withstood an earlier siege for seven years. Charles's guns breached the walls in four hours. In an exultant bulletin drawn up for printing and circulation back home, the king wrote that his troops had surged through the shattered ramparts of the fortress "in such a manner that, thanks to God, it has been taken with little loss to me, but to the defenders great loss, punishment, and great example to those others who might think of so obstructing me." Four months later, the king's guns were in action again, this time creating havoc in the ranks of an Italian army at Fornovo. Approximately 3,350 Italians were killed, compared with fewer than 200 Frenchmen.

After almost two centuries, artillery had finally come of age. The guns that were used in earlier campaigns had been large, clumsy, and unreliable, as likely to injure their operators as their targets. But the cannon developed by the French, manufactured from cast bronze, were light enough to travel on two-wheeled carriages, yet strong enough to withstand the pressure of gunpowder charges. Furthermore, they soon began to be mounted on trunnions, cylindrical projections just forward of the point of balance, which enabled them to be elevated to any angle, thus increasing the accuracy of their aim and range.

Significant improvements had also been made in handguns, a fact underlined with much blood in 1503, when the Spanish, intent on carving out their own slice of Italy, blasted an opposing French force off the field at Cerignola. Gunpowder was now poised to become the dominant factor in armed conflict, and over the next four centuries, its reverberations would echo through every continent. Not only would it enable the leading European powers to begin their domination of the world, but it would also bring to Europe itself more death, destruction, and despair than had all the wars of the previous three millennia.

The Chinese were the first to discover the explosive power of saltpeter, sulfur, and charcoal, and they began making use of the formula as early as the ninth century. Initially, gunpowder was used to propel rockets and to make incendiary and explosive projectiles thrown by catapults and trebuchets. By the thirteenth century, the Bureau of Munitions presided over seven factories with a combined work force of 40,000. In one day, they could produce 7,000 rockets and 21,000 bombs. Some, filled with arsenic or other lethal substances, released poisonous gas. Others, packed with tar and oil, burned like napalm. One of the deadliest weapons in the Chinese

Purporting to illustrate the battle between the Israelites and the Midianites recounted in the Bible in the Book of Judges, this miniature from a 1473 Flemish manuscript shows some of the miscellany of infantry weapons employed by late-fifteenth-century European armies: swords, pikes, bows, guns, and a form of hand-thrown bomb. Early hand-held guns, first used in Europe in the previous century, could not match the accuracy or range of the traditional bow and arrow, but improvements in design made the harquebus and later the musket the most deadly weapon on the battlefield. In 1490, the Venetian republic replaced all its crossbows with guns, having learned that even a small army equipped with gunpowder weapons held a winning advantage over a force that relied only on bows and pikes.

This seventeenth-century engraving of the Battle of Rain, fought in Germany in 1632 during the Thirty Years' War, shows the skillful deployment by the Swedish king Gustavus Adolphus of field artillery, cavalry, and infantry against the army of Count von Tilly. The advance of the Swedish cavalry across the Lech River is shielded by covering fire from field guns drawn up along the riverbank; in the foreground, infantry squares comprising pikemen surrounded by ranks of musketeers stand in reserve. This victory was won primarily by Gustavus's eighty light, mobile field guns, which could fire twenty rounds per hour.

arsenal was the "thunder-crash bomb," which having burst among the enemy troops, would then scatter them with vicious fragments of cast-iron casing.

Among those who suffered the effects of this last weapon were the Mongol troops besieging Kaifeng, capital of the Jin empire of northern China, in 1232. Although the Mongols eventually succeeded in capturing the city, they were forced to pay a heavy price for it. According to one of those trapped inside Kaifeng, "The assault became more and more fierce, so that the trebuchet stones flew through the air like rain. People said that they were like half-millstones or half-sledgehammers. The Jin defenders could not face them. But in the city, there were the kind of fire-missiles called

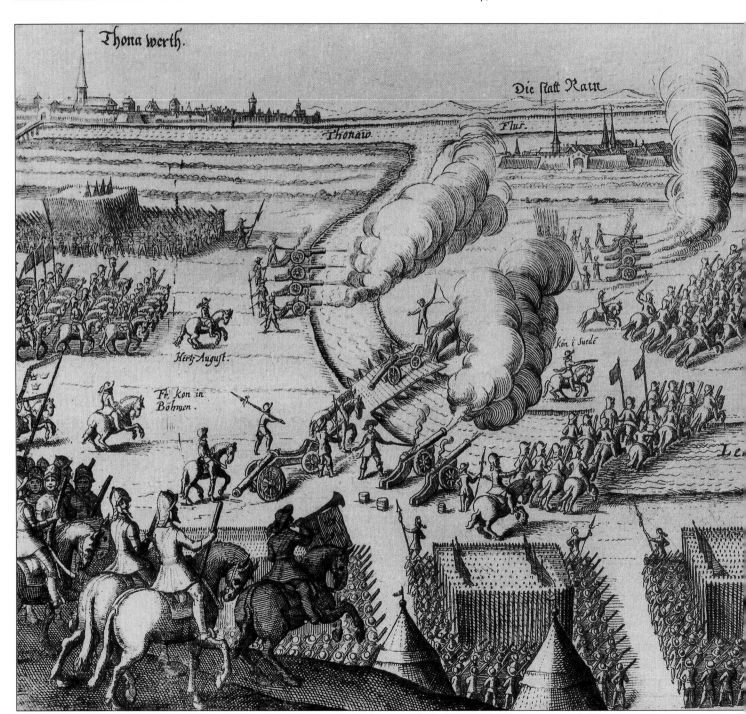

'heaven-shaking thunder-crash bombs,' and these were at last used in reply, so that the Mongol troops from the north suffered many casualties, and when not wounded by the explosions, were burned to death by the fires that they caused."

During the second half of the thirteenth century, the Chinese found an additional use for gunpowder: When ignited by means of touchholes, it would propel projectiles from metal barrels. It was around this time that gunpowder weapons also appeared in the Islamic world, although whether these were independently devised or copied from Chinese originals is unclear. In the West, the first-known recipe for gunpowder was written down in 1267 by Roger Bacon, an English cleric and scientist who taught in Paris and Oxford. Several of Bacon's colleagues were visitors to the Mongol court at Karakoram, and it seems that one of them returned bearing him a unique and fateful gift—a Chinese firecracker.

Knowledge of gunpowder was also spread by travelers returning from Arabia. The gunmakers of Europe would eventually outstrip those of China and, indeed, every other part of the civilized world. The Italian poet and scholar Petrarch, writing around 1350, observed that "these instruments that discharge balls of metal with most tremendous noise and flashes of fire . . . were a few years ago very rare and were viewed with greatest astonishment and admiration, but now they are become as common and familiar as any other kind of arms. So quick and ingenious are the minds of men in learning the most pernicious arts."

The early samples, however, were hardly impressive. Shaped like small pots and capable of discharging only arrowlike projectiles, they were far less effective than conventional missile weapons such as bows and slings. Although five of the new weapons are said to have been used by the English at the Battle of Crécy in 1346, they made little impression on the French, who were defeated by the lethal fire of the English longbowmen. The first breakthrough came with the introduction of tubular barrels. These produced far higher velocities than had previously been attainable, and instead of arrows, they fired masonry-shattering shot of iron or stone. The barrels were constructed either of wrought iron or cast bronze, the latter being the more popular since a bronze gun was cast in one piece and was less liable to burst than a gun of wrought-iron pieces welded together. Bellfounders proved adept at casting guns, and when the necessary metal was in short supply, the objects they had made for summoning the faithful to worship could be melted down and used for battering fortifications instead.

At this time, the overriding obsession was with size, and craftsmen strove to produce bigger and bigger weapons. The largest pieces were the aptly named bombards, which were often thirty inches or more in diameter and so heavy that they had to be hauled on ox-drawn sledges. According to the contemporary French chronicler Jean Froissart, Flemish rebels besieging the French-held fortress of Oudenaarde in 1382 "made a marvelous great bombard shooting stone of marvelous weight, and when this bombard shot, it made such a noise in the going as though all the devils of hell had been on the way."

The most spectacular use of artillery occurred in the year 1453, when the Ottoman sultan Mehmet II attacked the Byzantine capital of Constantinople. The sultan had retained the services of a renegade Hungarian gunmaker who produced seventy huge cannon for the assault, including a twenty-five-ton monster named Mahometta. This weapon was more than twenty-six feet long and was capable of firing stone balls up to 1,500 pounds in weight for a distance of almost one mile. So powerful was its discharge that pregnant women were said to have miscarried at the sound of it. Over a period of time, sections of Constantinople's huge ramparts began to crumble under the Turkish pounding, and on May 29, 1453, after a siege that had lasted fifty-four days, the city that had been the eastern bulwark of Christianity for more than a millennia fell at last before the attacking Muslims.

Giant guns, whatever their potential destructiveness, had severe limitations. Not only were they difficult to transport, but the process of reloading and repositioning them meant enormous delay between shots. Most of the Turkish cannon at Constantinople, for example, could only be fired every two hours. And the bigger the gun, the more likely it was to malfunction. The mighty Mahometta cracked on the second day of the siege and ceased working altogether by the end of the first week. Even more serious than cracking were the consequences of a gun blowing up. An early victim of rogue artillery was King James II of Scotland. In August 1460, while he was besieging Roxburgh Castle, one of his own bombards exploded, killing him and many of his followers.

In a detail from a Chinese silk banner of the tenth century, a demon with three serpents' heads rising from his hair wields a fire-lance—a tube packed with black powder, the first explosive invented—which could be used either as a flamethrower or to fire projectiles. In the foreground, a second demon prepares to hurl a casing bomb, which consisted of explosive powder wrapped in a ball of woven bamboo and paper that was lighted before being thrown. These two Chinese devices were the ancestors of all subsequent gunpowder weapons developed by Arab and European technicians.

The first to reverse the trend were the French, who found that several small cannon firing at relatively short intervals were much more effective than one lumbering bombard, firing a maximum of five or six times a day. The Florentine diplomat and historian Francesco Guicciardini, writing in the 1520s, observed that the guns used by Charles VIII's army "were planted against the walls of a town with such speed, the space between the shots was so little, and the balls flew so quickly and were impelled with such force, that as much execution was done in a few hours as formerly, in Italy, in the like number of days."

A second technical improvement also eagerly seized on by the French was the introduction of "corned" gunpowder. Because ordinary powder was extremely unstable, the least shaking was likely to make the heaviest element, the saltpeter, drop to the bottom and the carbon rise to the top. As a result, the powder often failed to burn, or burned so slowly as to lose its explosive effect. Some gunners overcame the problem by mixing their powder just before use—a process that was both time-consuming and dangerous. A better solution was to form the powder into small "corns," or grains, so that all three ingredients were exposed to the igniting flame at the same time. First, the powder had to be turned into a paste, and for this there were several fluids that could be used, including brandy and vinegar. By far the best, however, was said to be urine, especially that of a wine-drinking man.

The major effect of the new weaponry was to render all existing fortifications obsolete. "No wall exists, however thick," declared the Florentine philosopher and military theorist Niccolò Machiavelli in 1519, "that artillery cannot destroy in a few days." For centuries, military architects had tried to make defensive fortifications as high as possible, the main threat being that of escalade—an assault carried out with scaling ladders or siege towers. But height was now a positive disadvantage, since it merely offered the enemy gunners an easier target.

Architects and engineers therefore began to design walls that were both lower and thicker, with glancing surfaces that could deflect cannonballs. At the same time, angled bastions, or gun towers, were arranged at regular intervals around the perimeter of a fortress, not only giving the defenders an opportunity for flanking fire, but also enabling them to launch counterbarrages against attacking artillery. As cannon ranges improved, defenses became still more formidable, with many strongholds being surrounded by moats or ditches—these protected, in turn, by further fortifications. Faced with such resistance, a besieging force could look forward to a long and bloody war of attrition that might last for months or even years. As an Irish commander put it in the 1670s, "We make war more like foxes than like lions; and you will have twenty sieges for one battle."

On the battlefield itself, it was the handgun as well as the cannon that was now dictating events. Initially, there was no real difference between small arms and artillery pieces, except that the former could be carried and fired by a single individual. The problem was that the soldier wielding a firearm had to aim it at a target while also igniting the powder charge. In the 1450s, however, there appeared the harquebus, which was fired by a length of slow-burning match attached to a trigger. Although this was a considerable improvement over the primitive "fire-sticks" that had gone before, it still took several minutes to load, and its effective range of almost 250 feet was less than that of either the crossbow or the longbow. But it did have one great advantage: It required virtually no training for use. Unlike an archer, who had to develop a strong forearm in order to draw the bowstring, a harquebusier could learn how to load and fire his weapon after only a few days.

The first convincing demonstration that handguns could determine the outcome of a battle was the 1503 clash at Cerignola, where the charging French cavalry was mowed down by the mass fire of Spanish harquebusiers. The French, who were much slower than their opponents to realize the value of portable firearms, suffered another crushing defeat at Pavia in 1525. Here, the French king Francis I lost some 8,000 men, again most of them the victims of Spanish harquebusiers, and Francis himself was badly wounded and taken prisoner.

Even so, deadly as they might be, the first harquebusiers were no more than auxiliaries, employed as a protective fringe for the squares of traditional foot soldiers armed with shock weapons—usually pikes—who carried the main burden of the battle and who outnumbered the newcomers six to one. But the victory at Pavia convinced the Spaniards that firearms were an essential feature of modern warfare, and their infantry forces, organized as early as 1534 into 3,000-strong regiments known as *tercios,* included a substantial component of shot. At this point, however, the pikes protected the guns. Other countries also began to alter the ratio of pike and shot, but for a century to come, it was the tercio that remained unchallenged on the battlefields of Europe.

Spanish armies of a different kind dominated the newly discovered lands of Central and South America, although in this part of the world as well, gunpowder played a crucial role. In 1519, Hernán Cortés invaded the Aztec empire of Mexico with an expeditionary force that included approximately 500 soldiers, 32 harquebusiers, 7 small cannon, and 16 horses. By 1521, he had completely subjugated that huge country. Some of the Indians Cortés managed to win over as allies, but others preferred to fight. They were no match, however, for the firearms and cavalry of the conquistadors. Both the horse and the gun were new to the continent, and it was not unusual for Indian warriors to faint at the mere sound of discharging ordnance. Thus, in spite of being vastly outnumbered by their opponents, Cortés's troops were able to cut them down by the thousands.

The same grim story was to be repeated some ten years later when Francisco Pizarro, leading a force of only 180 soldiers, 27 horses, and 4 cannon, achieved the conquest of Peru. Pizarro's bloody progress was facilitated by the Indians' conviction that these bearded, steel-clad invaders were descendants of the Inca sun god. "This belief was much strengthened by the artillery and harquebuses the Spaniards had," wrote the sixteenth-century historian Garcilaso de la Vega—himself the son of an Inca princess—"for they said that the sun had armed them with its own weapons, as a father arms his sons. These weapons are lightning, thunder, and thunderbolts, which they call *illapa,* and they therefore applied this word to the harquebus. The artillery was given the same name with the adjective *hatun illapa,* meaning 'big thunder,' or 'big bolt.' "

Thus, armed like gods, the Spaniards were able to go about the devil's business in America. Over the succeeding centuries, all the nations of Europe were to follow suit, unleashing their thunderbolts in many parts of the world.

Gunpowder weapons were not only a threat to fortresses and armies; they also challenged a code of chivalry that held personal combat to be the indispensable test of knightly valor. "Would to heaven," lamented the sixteenth-century French commander Blaise de Montluc, who had himself been shot in the face by a harquebus, "that this accursed engine had never been invented. I had not then received those wounds that I now languish under, neither had so many valiant men been slain for the most part by the most pitiful fellows, and the greatest cowards . . . that had not dared to look those men in the face at hand, which at a distance they laid low with their confounded bullets."

Some expressed their scorn more forcibly. The redoubtable French general Pierre du Terrail, who served both Charles VIII and Francis I, ordered that all captured enemy gunners be summarily shot, while the veteran Italian commander Paolo Vitelli had them blinded and struck off their hands. It seemed, indeed, to many observers that gunpowder weapons, with their belching flames, sulfurous stench, and unprecedented destructive power, were tools of the devil.

The Church, which had tried unsuccessfully to ban the crossbow when it first appeared, was less dogmatic about the new weapons, arguing that those fighting for a just cause—in defense of Christendom against the infidels, for example—deserved to be at least as well-armed as their enemies. To remove any doubts on the matter, it provided gunners with their own patron saint, Saint Barbara. According to tradition, at the moment of the saint's execution, her father, who had denounced her to the pagan Romans, was struck down by thunder and lightning—righteous explosions that provided an unmistakable moral for her subsequent devotees. So popular did her cult become that the sixteenth-century Dutch scholar Erasmus was driven to deride the "foolish but gratifying belief that . . . whoever salutes an image of Barbara will come through a battle unscathed."

Nevertheless, even among the wielders of the new weaponry, old ideas of warfare persisted. During the years from 1598 to 1610, between 500 and 1,000 French aristocrats died as a result of duels. Even the Holy Roman Emperor Charles V and the French monarch Francis I (by now fully recovered from his wounds received at Pavia and released from captivity) were prevented from joining in single combat only by the intercession of the pope.

Any subsequent notions of recapturing the imagined chivalry that characterized medieval warfare were doomed by the introduction of the musket to European arsenals in the 1550s. A heavier version of the harquebus, it took longer to load and fire, and the barrel had to be supported on a forked rest that was stuck in the ground;

but it was capable of propelling a two-ounce lead shot with sufficient force to penetrate armor plate at a distance of about 260 feet, and so it posed a lethal threat to even the best-protected cavalry. For better or worse, the gun was to remain the unchallenged master of the battlefield.

Similar developments were transforming the nature of warfare at sea. Almost as soon as they had begun to hammer the city walls of Europe, guns had made their appearance on the decks of warships. These early fighting craft were low, slim galleys, powered by perhaps 150 oarsmen and designed for ramming enemy vessels. Although the guns on such ships could not be mounted to deliver a full broadside, they were successfully placed on platforms at the bow or stern. By the sixteenth century, a typical Venetian galley boasted eighteen guns, some of them capable of inflicting shattering damage.

According to an account of naval warfare that was published in 1614, the crew of a fighting ship had to become accustomed to the "havoc wrought among human limbs now by iron, now by fire (which is not so terrifying in land battles), the sight of this man torn to shreds and in the same moment burned up, another drowned, another pierced by a harquebus ball, yet another split into wretched pieces by the artillery. On top of this," the account continued, "there is the terror caused by the sight of a vessel swallowed up by the sea with all hands without the remotest possibility of rescue, to see the crew, half-alive, half-burned, sink miserably to the bottom while the sea changes color and turns red with human blood, covered the while with arms and with scraps and fragments of broken ships."

Because they were ideally suited to the still, summer waters of the Mediterranean, gun-bearing galleys remained swift and maneuverable enough to hold their own in battle against sailing ships until the middle of the seventeenth century. On the turbulent Atlantic Ocean, naval warfare took a different tack. During the second half of the fifteenth century, an increase in trade, along with an urge for exploration, demanded a vessel for all oceans and seasons, and it was the sailing ship that proved most adaptable to these longer, rougher voyages. A further advantage was that wind-powered craft called for only a fraction of the crew—and therefore the rations—required by galleys.

In addition, armed sailing ships had an obvious advantage over the traditional

A German firemaster holds a slow-burning stick, indispensable for the firing of all gunpowder devices until the invention of self-igniting weapons. The firemaster also held the upper hand in all negotiations for cash or food from villages that lay in the path of an advancing army: Behind the prancing horse in this engraving from a 1598 treatise on war, panic-stricken civilians can be seen fleeing from a burning village that has not acceded to the demands of the firemaster.

69

MAXIMIZING FIREPOWER

Gunpowder opened the military armory to weapons potentially more deadly than those used previously, but the problems of harnessing its explosive power took time to solve. Many early inventors overreached themselves, devising weapons whose practicality did not match their ambition, as shown here and overleaf. But in the process, they unwittingly created the prototypes of weapons that subsequent technology would render more feasible, such as the machine gun and the tank. And when they concentrated on fundamental details, such as the firing mechanism, they made considerable advances.

A basic problem of a gun packed with powder lighted directly through a touchhole was that it could not be loaded, aimed, and fired by a single soldier. The solution devised in the mid-fifteenth century was the matchlock, a pivoting S-shape bar on the side of the gun threaded with a slow-burning cord. A soldier could now aim the gun on a rest and immediately fire by pulling the cord's free end, thus lowering the lighted end onto the touchhole.

The matchlock remained the most efficient mechanism until the introduction in the late sixteenth century of the flintlock, in which the powder was ignited by a spark from a flint in a triggered hammer. By this time, other improvements—such as the spiral grooving of the barrel to improve accuracy and the shaping of the stock to minimize the impact of recoil—were also combining to make the powder-filled tube an ever-more-lethal instrument.

A bristling German war chariot in a watercolor dated 1505 is armed with four light cannon barrels. While one gun is fired, a fifth barrel—detached from the chariot—is reloaded by its attendant.

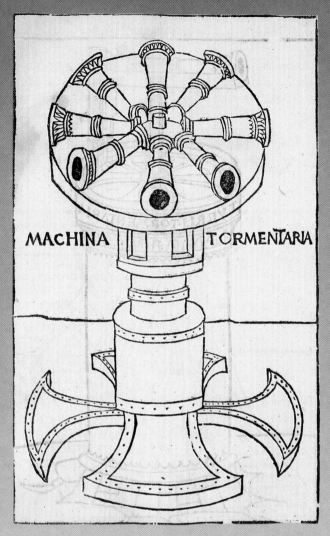

MACHINA TORMENTARIA

In a 1483 Italian woodcut, a turntable mounted on a chest-high stand holds eight barrels that can be fired in rapid succession. The risk of all barrels being fired simultaneously by a stray spark made this device as dangerous to its own gunners as it was to the enemy.

A prototype machine gun patented in England in 1718 has a single, fixed barrel and a rotating magazine that can be locked in position to fire each cylinder by a flintlock mechanism. The inventor offered two magazines: one containing round shot, for use against Christian enemies, the other with square shot—causing more terrible wounds—for non-Christians.

The three upper guns in this 1505 painting (left) each comprise four short barrels mounted on a single wooden support—one barrel of the third example is being fired by application of a flame to the touchhole. The bottom gun, equipped with three barrels and supported by a hand-held rest, was fired by a matchlock mechanism: The top of the S-shape bar that held a slow-burning fuse is seen near the center of the gun.

fighting galley: They could be equipped with guns all along their sides. At first, cannon were placed on the upper deck and on the high wooden superstructures—the so-called castles—that towered both fore and aft. Since heavy guns situated in such a manner tended to make a vessel perilously top-heavy, however, warships came to be equipped with hinged gunports cut into their hulls. This innovation, dating from 1500, meant that artillery could be installed on two or more levels, transforming the sailing ship into a floating fortress.

Some of the new warships built to maximize firepower were grossly misconceived. England's king Henry VIII was an enthusiastic proponent of naval gunnery, but a number of the grandiose products of his shipyards proved virtually useless. His 1,300-ton *Henri Grâce à Dieu,* for instance, carried 184 guns, more than twice the capacity of many contemporary warships, but its lack of maneuverability and huge running costs made it a monument to the king's inflated ambitions. The *Mary Rose,* weighing 780 tons and carrying 78 guns, actually keeled over and sank with all hands while sailing against the French in 1545.

Despite these setbacks, King Henry oversaw a revolution in the design of naval ordnance that would launch England as Europe's leading sea power. Instead of equipping English ships with the traditional two-wheeled field guns, Henry and his advisers mounted their naval pieces on compact truck carriages that had four small wheels. Lacking the space-consuming wooden brace, or trail, that extended out behind conventional artillery, these specially built naval cannon could be hauled back from the gunports after firing, quickly reloaded, and then positioned to fire again. A gunnery crew, which was trained to work as a team, attended each cannon during an engagement.

Unfortunately, Henry did not live to see the triumphant vindication of his policy. Instead, it was his formidable daughter Elizabeth I who saw it come to fruition. In the summer of 1588, a huge Spanish fleet, known as the Armada, sailed into the English Channel. Had its nearly 30,000 well-armed soldiers and sailors successfully landed on the Kent coast, there is every likelihood that they might have carried out their objective of conquering England. As it was, they encountered an enemy that fought at sea by an entirely new set of rules. Over the previous three decades, the bulky warships of Henry's era had been replaced or rebuilt. Lower and sleeker, outfitted with heavier guns and more efficient sails, the galleons of the Elizabethan navy were among the best in Europe.

Not only did the English have more ships than their opponents, they also had about 30 percent more cannon—and they insisted on using them in their own way. During more than one week of intermittent fighting, the Spaniards were unsuccessful in their attempts to grapple and board the enemy ships, a tactic that, given their huge numerical superiority, would have assured them of victory. Instead, they were subjected to rapid and close-range cannon fire, which blasted holes in their ships and reduced the Spaniards to frustrated rage. At one point, the captain of the shattered galleon *San Felipe* shouted out to his tormentors to come alongside and fight like men. The English vessel wisely declined the invitation. That night, the *San Felipe* ran aground on the sandbars of Flanders—only 127 of the 457 men who had sailed on the ship managed to reach dry land.

While weather and courage and fortune all played a part in the outcome, the pivotal factor in the English defeat of the Armada was the cannon. Although the Spanish guns were powerful, their long trails prevented the crews from loading them quickly enough to make any impression on the English. While Admiral Lord Charles Howard's fleet had run dangerously short of both powder and shot by August 8, the climactic day of the battle, the duke of Medina-Sidonia's ships had scarcely begun to use their supply. Poignant evidence of this fact has come to light in recent decades as a result of undersea explorations. Among the storm-wrecked remains of the Spanish galleons that litter the rocky seafloors off Scotland and Ireland lie scattered scores of unused cannonballs.

The defeat of the Spanish Armada did not signal the immediate demise of cumbersome ships or old-fashioned hand-to-hand battles at sea. But it did indicate a direction in which at least some were eager to follow. In 1618, the English naval board commissioners succinctly summarized the lessons that would be gradually absorbed over the following century:

> Experience teacheth how sea fights in these days come seldom to boarding or to great execution of bows, arrows, small shot, and the swords, but are chiefly performed by the great artillery breaking down masts, yards, tearing, raking, and bilging the ships, wherein the great advantage of His Majesty's navy must carefully be maintained by appointing such a proportion of ordnance to each ship as the vessel will bear.

On land, as on sea, going into combat under a murderous hail of lead demanded a new code of conduct for the combatants. In addition to the ferocity necessary to charge enemy lines, the modern soldier now required the fortitude to remain unflinching under fire. One such soldier was the French monarch Henry IV, whose battlefield demeanor was described by an admiring Venetian ambassador in 1598. The king, he wrote, "moves fearlessly under harquebus and cannon fire without giving it a thought and as gaily as if he were going to a wedding." An extreme example of sang-froid in the heat of action occurred during the 1582 siege of Oudenaarde, near Brussels. One afternoon, the commander of the besieging Spanish, the duke of Parma, had a table set near the trenches so he and his staff could dine in the open air. Hardly had the meal commenced when a ball flew over the table, taking off the head of a young officer, a fragment of whose skull struck out the eye of one of his neighbors. A second ball dispatched two more of the duke's guests. With blood and brains now liberally scattered over the table, the duke remained unruffled. Having seen to the removal of the corpses and ordered a fresh tablecloth, he requested everyone to resume their places and continue eating.

Eccentric acts of personal bravery did not win wars, however. What was needed was a means of instilling whole armies with an unthinking capacity to perform mundane tasks—to load and fire and reload—in the face of death. The solution was found by Prince Maurice of Nassau, who in 1584 was appointed to lead the United Provinces of the Netherlands in their struggle for independence against Spain. Inspired by the disciplined battlefield tactics of the ancient Romans rather than by the chaotic free-for-alls of medieval Europeans, Maurice insisted on regular and repetitive rehearsals of the most fundamental military tasks. While other European commanders considered their troops prepared if they could fire and recharge their muskets with reasonable speed, Maurice demanded far greater precision and competence. He equipped his entire army with identical muskets and insisted that each man be trained to use his weapon according to the drill manual prepared by his cousin, Count John. This remarkable book, which quickly went into Danish, German, French, and English editions, described thirty-two positions for the pikeman and forty-two for the musketeer.

Maurice further increased his troops' rate of fire by borrowing another idea from the Romans. This was the countermarch, originally designed for javelin and slingshot throwers. As adapted by the Dutch, the first rank of musketeers would fire a volley and then retire to reload in the rear while the following ranks came forward and repeated the process. Provided each rank followed the prescribed pattern, the enemy would be subjected to a continuous barrage of shot. The faster a commander's men were able to perform this maneuver, the fewer ranks he would need and the longer he could extend his line of battle.

Prince Maurice's campaigns were devoted more to sieges than to battlefield encounters, and it was the Swedish king Gustavus Adolphus who brought the idea of volley fire to practical fruition. He ascended the throne in 1611 at the age of seventeen and was engaged in campaigns for most of his twenty-one-year reign. By the time he marched into Germany in 1630 to fight against the Hapsburgs and their Catholic allies in the savage religious conflict that came to be known as the Thirty Years' War, he was a seasoned commander at thirty-five, leading an experienced army consisting of native Swedes and foreign mercenaries.

Gustavus drilled his troops in the Dutch fashion, perfecting Prince Maurice's techniques until an infantry line only six ranks deep could keep up a continuous fire while advancing toward the enemy. The development of powder and ball encased in paper cartridges speeded reloading, and the introduction of lighter firearms that no longer required a support made it easier for the musketeers—who now outnumbered the pikemen by two to one—to go through their maneuvers. Under Gustavus's direction, most of the existing Swedish artillery was called in to the armorers and recast as light and highly mobile field pieces. Each regiment of 1,000 men was issued four three-pounders, which could easily keep up with an army on the march and could fire up to twenty rounds an hour—almost as fast as a musketeer.

In September 1631, on a field known as God's Acre near the village of Breitenfeld, north of Leipzig, Gustavus Adolphus faced a Hapsburg army under the command of the fierce and experienced Count von Tilly. The two sides made a striking contrast. Tilly drew up his infantry in the tercio formations that had been perfected by Spain more than a century earlier, while Gustavus deployed his foot soldiers in six ranks behind a formidable array of artillery. It was a test of the old tactics against the new. Raked by the Swedish guns, which were more numerous and could fire at three times the speed of their own, Tilly's army nevertheless gained a temporary advantage when the Swedes' untested Saxon allies fled the field in panic. The Swedish reserve marched promptly forward to take their places, however, and the Hapsburg forces went down in catastrophic defeat.

Having driven Tilly and his men from their positions, Colonel Robert Monro, commander of Gustavus's Scottish brigade, wrote:

> We were masters of their cannon, and consequently of the field, but the smoke being great and the dust being raised, we were as in a dark cloud, not seeing the half of our actions, much less discerning either the way of our enemies or yet the rest of our brigades: Whereupon, having a drummer by me, I caused him to beat the Scots march, till it cleared up, which

recollected our friends unto us . . . so that the brigade coming together, such as were alive, missed their dead and hurt comrades.

Gustavus lost some 3,000 men, but Tilly lost 12,000—almost one-third of his army—and a further 7,000 were captured.

Although Gustavus never lived to see it—he was shot dead at the Battle of Lützen in Saxony only one year after his triumph at Breitenfeld—his methods were copied by other European powers, the most notable of which was France. During the second half of the seventeenth century, the French army developed from an impoverished rabble into a well-trained force numbering almost 300,000, the largest such body since the days of the Roman Empire. Under the leadership of two remarkable bureaucrats, Michel Le Tellier and his son, the marquis de Louvois, many of the reforms initiated by Prince Maurice and King Gustavus Adolphus were brought into effect on a grand scale. From that time on, all potential officers were required to train as musketeers in the Royal Guard. A horde of civilian officials oversaw the complexities of providing the troops with food, pay, equipment, and shelter. And to ensure that drill and discipline were effectively enforced, Louvois appointed as his inspector general Jean Martinet, a man whose name subsequently was to become synonymous with rigid adherence to rules.

In the 1690s, Europe's armies began to equip themselves with the new flintlock musket. A smoothbore muzzleloader, but lighter than the matchlock it replaced, the flintlock's main advantage was its improved rate of fire. Pulling the trigger released a piece of flint that was held in a spring-loaded vice. This hammered down on a metal surface, creating the spark that ignited the powder. According to one manual, doing away with the smoldering fuse reduced the number of steps that were required to fire a musket from forty-four to twenty-six. A well-drilled regiment could now discharge two or even three rounds a minute, almost twice the previous rate. In spite of the increased firepower capability, however, the flintlock was not a particularly accurate weapon: At a distance of about 600 feet, well within its range, a musketeer could rarely be sure of hitting his target. But the lead ball, which left the muzzle at more than 980 feet per second and could rip through a pine post almost five inches thick, inflicted fearful damage on an enemy within 150 feet.

The turn of the century also brought the development of the socket bayonet, which made the musket a truly all-purpose weapon. The earlier plug bayonet had not been entirely successful, since once it was fixed into the musket's muzzle, it prevented the musketeers from firing their weapons. The victory of the Highland Scots over the English at Killiecrankie in 1689 was ascribed by General Hugh Mackay, the defeated commander, to the fact that the "Highlanders are of such quick motion that if a battalion keep up its fire until they be near to make sure of hitting them, they are upon it before our men can come to the second defense, which is the bayonet in the muzzle of the musket." But with

A seventeenth-century English engraving *(below)* shows a musketeer ready for battle with all his equipment stashed about him. In his right hand, he holds a rest for the musket's barrel; from his left hand, gripping the gun's stock, dangles a cord for threading into the matchlock firing mechanism. The photograph below the engraving shows the bandoleer slung across the musketeer's chest in closeup: Suspended from it are a leather pouch containing pellets for the musket and nine cylindrical wooden cartridges, each of which held the correct amount of powder for firing one shot.

March with ÿ Rest in your Right Hand

the introduction of the socket bayonet, which fit around the musket's muzzle, the soldier could be firing at one instant and stabbing at the next.

The musketeer, provided now with his own means of protection, had no further need of the pike. The French abandoned it in 1703, the English the following year. By 1710, nearly all the infantrymen in Europe were equipped with the musket and socket bayonet. The latter was, in fact, more a threat than a real danger. Some officers, like the English general Burgoyne, continued to insist that "the bayonet in the hands of the valiant is irresistible." But the valiant had few opportunities to fight at close quarters. "Firearms are the most destructive category of weapon," observed the marquis de Puysegur, who served in the French army from 1677 to 1735. "If you need convincing," he wrote in his *Art of War,* "just go to the hospital, and you will see how few men have been wounded by cold steel as opposed to firearms."

Such casualties derived little comfort from the ministrations of military surgeons, many of whom joined the army because they had failed to obtain employment in civilian life. Even coming under the care of a skilled doctor was of little help. Until the early nineteenth century, it was common practice to cauterize gunshot wounds with boiling oil and to apply a red-hot iron to the stump left by the amputation of a shattered limb. In either case, the patient was as likely to die of shock as to recover. Anesthetics were still unknown, and often an injured soldier preferred a quick death at the hands of a comrade to the lingering agonies of a field hospital. After fighting between the French and Italians in 1536, an eminent French physician, Ambroise Paré, saw three men horribly burned by gunpowder. "Beholding them with pity," he wrote, "there came an older soldier who asked me if there was any means of curing them. I told him no. At once he approached them and cut their throats gently, and seeing this great cruelty, I shouted at him that he was a villain. He answered me that he prayed to God that when he should be in such a state he might find someone who would do the same for him, to the end that he might not languish miserably."

In this sixteenth-century engraving of an engagement in the Mediterranean Sea between an oar-powered galley and a galleon under full sail, smoke billows from the cannon ranged along both sides of the galleon. Galleys had ruled the Mediterranean since the time of the ancient Greeks, but ships armed with cannon could usually prevent them from coming close enough to ram or send boarding parties onto their opponents. The cutting of hinged gunports in the sides of sailing ships around 1500 enabled them to fire broadsides, and by sailing in an extended line, an entire fleet could bring its firepower to bear on an enemy at the same time.

A greater killer than either flying lead or the knife of the surgeon was illness. Because they were poorly fed, sheltered, and clothed, and frequently obliged to live in the open without shelter or sanitation, the soldiers of this period were prey to a host of infections, such as influenza, typhus, typhoid, malaria, and dysentery. Heat, thirst, and exhaustion also claimed their share of victims, and it was not unusual for soldiers to drop dead on the march.

Since most knew little of the cause for which they fought, and many were mercenaries, troops were inclined to desert when conditions became especially bad. Subsequently, they would scavenge the local countryside, friendly or hostile, widening still further the chasm that existed between civilians and the military. Soldiers, indeed, were generally regarded as pariahs—agents of criminality, disorder, and disease. Certainly, it was not unknown for the violence of the battlefield to be transferred to the streets. In 1550, for example, the City of London was thrown into panic by an influx of discharged veterans returning from the Continent. "There be such a number of soldiers at this present within this city," wrote an anguished official, "that unless speedy order be taken to rid and bestow them into the country, great danger will thereby ensue." The men were disgruntled at not being able to obtain work and were threatening to "meet all together in some one place in the said city and thereupon set upon the citizens and their houses and take there such booties and spoil . . . they can lay hand upon." In 1537, the French authorities, facing similar problems, imposed the death penalty for any demobilized soldier who did not head directly for his own home.

The only Oriental power that was capable of challenging the West's military ascendancy in the age of gunpowder was Ottoman Turkey. After capturing Constantinople, vast Ottoman armies had won a string of victories in the Balkans, North Africa, and the Middle East and posed a continual threat to Christendom's southeastern frontier. Early evidence that the Turks were vulnerable occurred during battles at sea, however. In 1571, in the Battle of Lepanto, a European fleet of galleys and galleasses—heavy warships equipped with both sails and oars—annihilated the Ottoman navy, sinking or capturing more than 200 vessels and killing about 30,000 of the enemy. The key to victory was firepower. Although they were outnumbered in ships by the Ottomans, the Europeans mounted twice as many guns as the other side. Furthermore, the Turks ran out of ammunition even for the cannon they did possess, and some Ottoman crew members were reduced to pelting their opponents with oranges and lemons. "You have shaved off our beard," the sultan's chief minister told the Venetian ambassador, "but it will grow again." And so it did. By the following year, the huge Ottoman fleet had been rebuilt. Many of its cannon were so poorly cast, however, as to be ineffective.

On land, too, the Turks were ill-served by their artillery. Unlike the Europeans, they retained their passion for giant guns, thinking perhaps that the descendants of the monstrous pieces that had toppled the walls of Constantinople would likewise deliver the other great cities of Christendom into their hands. In fact, the opposite was the case. General Raimundo Montecuccoli, who routed an Ottoman army at the Battle of Szentgotthard in 1664, wrote that their "enormous artillery produces great damage when it hits, but it is awkward to move, and it requires too much time to reload and sight. Furthermore, it consumes a great amount of powder besides cracking and breaking the wheels and the carriages and even the ramparts on which it is

Embrasures and casements cut into the the walls of this English fort—one of twenty-eight built by Henry VIII in the 1530s to defend his southern coast—enable defenders to return a besieger's artillery fire equally. The semicircular bays afforded all-around protection, but their hollow structure rendered them less immune to enemy bombardment than the solid, angular bastions that were being constructed elsewhere in Europe.

THE SCIENCE OF THE SIEGE

As medieval walls crumbled under the impact of the siege artillery of the gunpowder age, military engineers hastened to devise more sturdy defenses. The first priority was to build thick, squat walls that were difficult both to breach and to undermine. But as the characteristic effects of artillery fire became more clearly understood, the planning of fortifications became an increasingly sophisticated discipline.

Because a cannonball splintered even when it did not breach a stone wall, earth ramparts—which absorbed artillery fire like a sponge—were used as backfill for stone or brick walls. It was also noted that a shot fired across an enemy line was far more effective than a direct frontal barrage: Not only was precise accuracy of range less important, but as the shot ricocheted across the ground—like a flat stone skipping across water—it cut a longer swath of destruction. In the early sixteenth century, Italian architects pioneered the construction of angled bastions projecting from short curtain walls: As well as being solidly constructed, and thus virtually impossible to knock down, they offered improved opportunities for cross fire and were widely copied throughout Europe.

Every improvement devised by defenders was matched by equal ingenuity on the part of attackers, however, as illustrated in this diagram (below). As a consequence, many sieges continued for months, or even for years, and were terminated only by starvation within the besieged town.

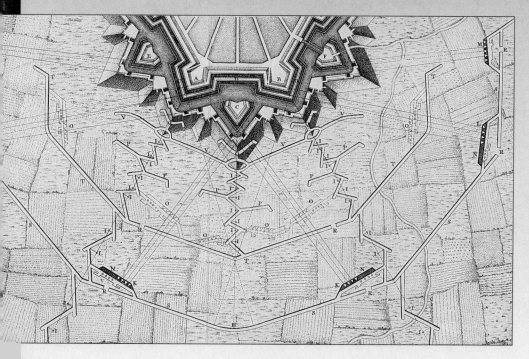

A detail from a treatise on siege warfare by the seventeenth-century French military engineer Sébastien Le Prestre de Vauban shows preparations for besieging a fort with angled bastions. A zigzagging network of trenches protects assault troops approaching the walls; behind them, siege guns are aligned to fire the length of the angled walls, destroying the guns stationed atop the bastions.

placed. . . . Our artillery is more handy to move and more efficient, and here resides our advantage over the cannon of the Turks."

Twenty years later, the Ottomans' obsession with size again turned to their disadvantage. Besieging Vienna in 1683, they were defeated by a relieving army, in part because they were unable to haul their heavy siege guns around in time to face the enemy. From then on, the Turks suffered a series of setbacks. A century after its defeat at the gates of Vienna, the mighty empire's grandiose weaponry and obsolete tactics were more likely to inspire amusement than terror in the courts of Europe. "It is not valor, numbers, or wealth that they lack; it is order, discipline, and technique," declared the great French commander Marshal de Saxe in 1732.

As war in Europe became ever more costly and destructive, scholars subjected it to intensive study, launching a flood tide of speculation on its causes, nature, and effects. An early contributor to the debate was the shrewd and cynical Machiavelli, who distilled his observations into two of the most influential books of all time—*The Prince* and *On the Art of War*. In his view, aggression was an ineradicable part of the human condition, and the appearance of gunpowder weapons simply made all the more urgent the need for a regimented form of society that would regulate and control human beings' destructive urges.

Machiavelli's Dutch contemporary Erasmus took the opposite view, condemning war as wicked and unnatural. "Whoever heard of a hundred thousand animals rushing together to butcher each other as men do everywhere?" he demanded. And could someone be "even minutely sensitive about killing one person when mass murder is his profession?" Warfare turned human values upside down. "Among the soldiers," he railed, "the one who has conducted himself with the most savagery is the one who is thought worthy to be captain in the next war."

Equally outspoken was Erasmus's compatriot, the jurist and theologian Hugo Grotius. "I saw prevailing throughout the Christian world," wrote Grotius in 1625, "a license in making war of which even barbarous nations would have been ashamed." The solution to the problem of indiscriminate killing, which he advocated in his masterwork *On the Law of War and Peace,* was to understand the natural laws that underlay all social behavior. "In the midst of divergent opinions," he wrote, "we must lean toward peace." There were times, however, when war was inevitable—in which case it "should be tempered with humanity, lest by imitating wild beasts too much we forget to be human."

Grotius, in fact, had troubles enough of his own. In 1613, he became involved in a bitter religious controversy that brought him into conflict with the Dutch leader Prince Maurice of Nassau. Imprisoned for life in Loevestein castle, Grotius escaped, hidden in a chest supposedly containing books. "I thought that they could never keep him in prison," Maurice remarked upon hearing of his prisoner's escape, "for he was wiser than all his judges." Exiled from his native land, Grotius accepted a post as a diplomat for Sweden, whose monarch, Gustavus Adolphus, was one of his many admirers. A copy of *On the Law of War and Peace* was found in Gustavus's tent on the day that most martial of rulers was killed in battle.

Many thinkers adopted a more extreme stance than that of Grotius. Talk of humanity in war, they argued, was mere hypocrisy. All war was evil, and the only worthwhile objective was its total and permanent abolition. "We must abandon these barbaric habits and show mankind the way of humanity and true honor," wrote

Émeric Cruce, a French monk, who in 1623 published his plan for a worldwide assembly of nations with the power to raise an international peacekeeping force. Similar proposals continued to surface throughout the next two centuries. William Penn, the wellborn Quaker whose ''holy experiment'' in Pennsylvania briefly came close to achieving his hope for a peaceable domain, envisaged a united Europe in which each nation would be allocated representation in proportion to its wealth. Voting would be secret and the debating chamber round, with several doors, so as to avoid any squabbles over precedence.

Many of the same ideas were put forward by the French cleric Abbé de Saint-Pierre. His *Project for Perpetual Peace,* first published in 1713, gave each nation one vote in an international senate whose decisions would be binding. When negotiations failed, a refractory member state would find itself facing an international army—the only time the harmonious powers would have recourse to war.

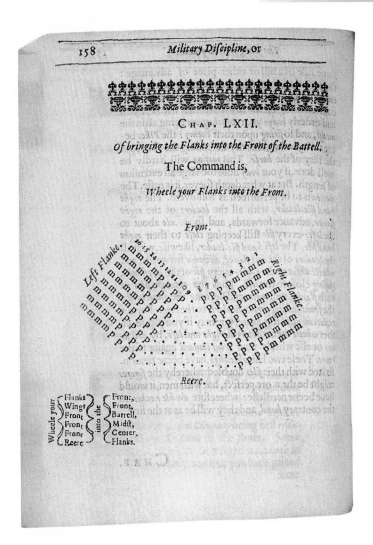

A page from an English drill manual of 1635 illustrates the maneuver for turning an infantry company's flanks—here made up of sixty-four musketeers, designated by the letter *m*—to the front, thereby positioning the central ranks of pikemen *(p)* in the rear. Continual drill practice was essential to ensure that soldiers obeyed commands quickly and proficiently during the press and din of battle. At the end of the maneuver shown here, the musketeers would be positioned to maintain a volley of fire—the front rank reloading as the second rank advanced to fire—while their rear was protected by the pikemen.

Beguiling as they were to the moralists and visionaries on the Continent, such schemes were greeted with absolutely no enthusiasm in those places where the issues of peace and war were actually decided—the royal palaces of Europe. Frederick the Great, the astute and bellicose king of Prussia, encapsulated the problem in an ironic letter to the French philosopher Voltaire. "The thing is most practicable," he wrote of Saint-Pierre's *Project*. "For its success, all that is lacking is the consent of Europe and a few similar trifles."

Frederick, who reigned from 1740 to 1786, was himself a master of the military arts, and under his ceaseless prompting, the Prussian army was turned into the most efficient fighting machine that existed in Europe. It was also subject to the harshest discipline. "If a soldier during an action looks about as if to flee, or so much as sets foot outside the line," the king wrote in 1745, "the noncommissioned officer standing behind him will run him through with his bayonet and kill him on the spot." As Frederick later elaborated, since obeying certain commands meant facing death, soldiers "must fear their officers more than any danger." Above all, the ordinary soldier must never be allowed to think. "No one reasons; everyone executes," he observed on another occasion.

Lessons that had been learned on the parade ground, however, were liable to be forgotten during the smoke and confusion that accompanied battle. With men—or pieces of men—falling all around and shouted commands unheard above the roar of guns and the screaming of cannon shot, a soldier's instinct was to fire as quickly as possible. But this increased the chances of hitting a comrade who was standing in one of the forward ranks, and many men fell with wounds in the back while bravely facing the enemy.

Even fire that was aimed in the right direction was often wildly inaccurate. Prussian and English muskets were not provided with sights, and there was no command for "take aim" in the otherwise elaborate Prussian loading drill. It was simply assumed that a hail of lead balls would hit human flesh when aimed generally at a mass of approaching bodies. A good volley, it was reckoned, would take one life for every 200 rounds, but the wastage rate was sometimes twice that. Everyone who survived a battle unscathed had inevitably escaped dozens of near misses. Lord Balcarres, who commanded the British infantry at Fort Ticonderoga during the American Revolution, emerged from the battle with thirty bullet holes in his uniform but only one slight graze on his hip.

The most terrifying battlefield experience was probably the artillery barrage. Fired on a low trajectory and at a slightly oblique angle to the enemy line, a solid iron cannonball, or so-called round shot, would do most of its damage as it ricocheted across the ground, tripling or even quadrupling its flight distance and wounding or killing all those who stood in its path. For shorter range work, at 650 feet or less, there was case shot, consisting of a tin canister that sprayed the enemy with small lead balls as soon it left the muzzle. The short-barreled howitzer, which lobbed explosive shells, was favored for setting fire to buildings and for panicking cavalry formations. Eight to ten horses, it was said, could be brought down by one well-directed shell.

To a Russian under fire from Frederick the Great's cannon at Zorndorf in 1758, it seemed "as if heaven and earth had fallen in on themselves." On the same day, but on the other side of the field, a Prussian lieutenant experienced the horror of the Russian cannonade: "My flank man's head was blown off," he later recalled, "and his brains flew in my face." From the safety of the guns themselves, the picture could look quite different. "I had a fine situation for galling the French army as they marched to the attack in columns . . .," gloated an English artillery officer on the Caribbean island of Saint Lucia in 1778. "My shot in this situation swept them off by the dozens at a time, and Frenchmen's heads were as plenty and cheaper than sheep's heads and trotters in Scotland."

Yet even in the gunpowder age, there were times when opponents preferred chivalry to butchery. In December 1757, for example, when French and German soldiers found themselves camped on opposite sides of a river, the former were allowed across to gather firewood. "A Hanoverian post was stationed at the actual barrier," recalled the French commander, "but it let us continue our work with a benevolence that was agreeable to see. The enemy sentry asked me for some tobacco, which was passed to him hand to hand by our workers, and his officer duly raised his hat to me."

A few months later, it was the turn of a British officer to be impressed by the magnanimity of the French. They were, he wrote, "a very generous enemy and above taking little advantages. I myself am an instance of it, among many that happen almost daily. Being out a-coursing a few days ago, I was galloping at full speed after a hare that we found, into a thicket where they had a post of infantry, and must infallibly have been taken prisoner if the officer commanding had not showed himself and very genteelly called out to stop me. We frequently discourse together."

Such courtesies, however, were to become extremely rare during the twenty-five years of savage conflict that followed the French Revolution in 1789. This conflict had little influence on weapons or even tactics, but it gave rise to a powerful new weapon—nationalism. Suddenly, the French state had become the French nation, whose citizens eagerly sprang to its defense against the invading armies of its enemies. Declared the French National Convention in August 1793:

> *From this moment until that when the enemy is driven from the territory of the republic, every Frenchman is permanently requisitioned for the needs of the armies. The young men will go to the front; the married men will forge arms and carry food; the women will make tents and clothing and work in hospitals; the children will turn old linen into bandages; the old men will be carried into the squares to rouse the courage of the combatants and to teach hatred of kings and the unity of the republic.*

The response of the French people was overwhelming. Almost overnight, weapons factories seemed to sprout in the gardens and parks of Paris, and the city rapidly became the largest producer of small arms in the world. Instructions for gathering saltpeter were broadcast throughout the country, and two citizens from each district were summoned to the capital to be trained in the casting of ordnance and the manufacture of gunpowder. The army, which had stood at around 150,000 in 1789,

As European military and naval power was converted to economic advantage—especially in the Americas, India, Southeast Asia, and Africa—each nation's furtherance of its own ambitions brought it into conflict with native armies, with rival European powers, and sometimes with its own independent-minded colonists. This map (below) shows the global reach of these conflicts up to the year 1789. The European military presence abroad—reinforced by locally recruited troops such as the Indian sepoy (opposite)—foreshadowed the amassing of colonial empires in the nineteenth century. It also ensured that thenceforth, a local conflict was liable to involve the interests of many different nations.

numbered almost 750,000 by 1794. For the most part, these volunteers were untrained, and at first some were armed only with pikes, since there were not enough muskets to go around.

Whatever these raw recruits lacked in skill, however, they made up for in zeal. Love of country, which was a consideration that did not appear in the eighteenth-century military textbooks, could now turn the tide of battle. "No more maneuvers, no more military art, but fire, steel, and patriotism!" declared Lazare Carnot, organizer of the revolutionary forces.

Such were the troops with which Napoleon Bonaparte challenged the rest of Europe. An artillery officer by training, Napoleon had been taught by the chevalier

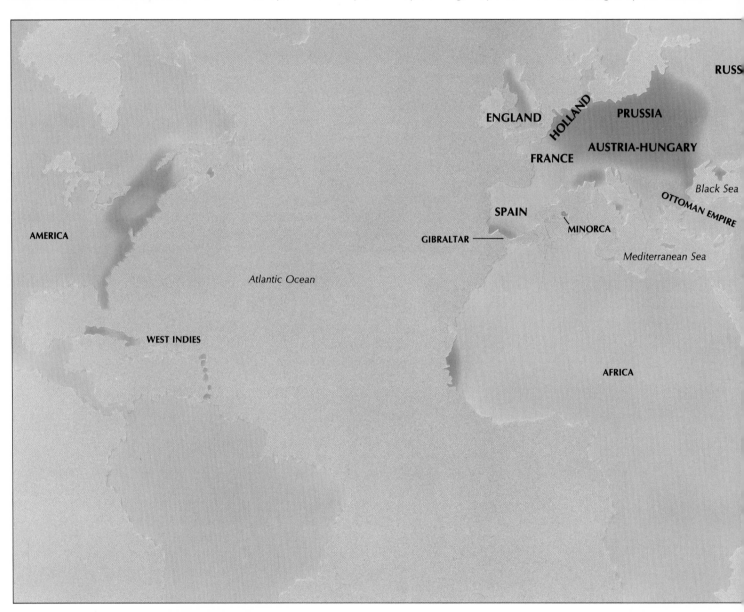

RUSS

ENGLAND HOLLAND PRUSSIA

AUSTRIA-HUNGARY

FRANCE

Black Sea

OTTOMAN EMPIRE

SPAIN

MINORCA

GIBRALTAR

Mediterranean Sea

AMERICA

Atlantic Ocean

WEST INDIES

AFRICA

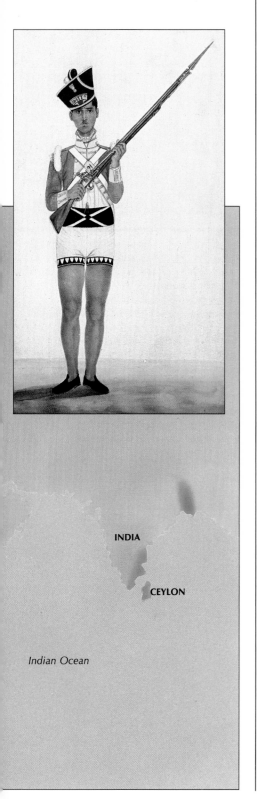

INDIA

CEYLON

Indian Ocean

Jean du Teil, who was a firm advocate of firepower. "We must collect the greatest number of troops and a greater quantity of artillery at the point where we wish to break the enemy," advised du Teil in his artillery manual written in 1778. These tactics suited Napoleon perfectly. He encouraged the use of light infantry, sending forward waves of skirmishers to disrupt his formally trained opponents before his main army—which was deployed in large, swiftly moving columns and covered by devastating artillery fire—overwhelmed them at their weakest point. The results were astonishing. With the crucial exception of Great Britain, defended by its navy, the countries that found themselves opposed to Napoleon crumbled before the speed and intensity of his advance.

For a man who fully understood the power of artillery, however, the French emperor took surprisingly little interest in musketry training. Indeed, Gouvion-Saint-Cyr, one of Napoleon's marshals, later estimated that 25 percent of all French infantry casualties during the Napoleonic Wars were caused by men in the front rank being accidentally shot by those in the ranks behind.

By contrast, Napoleon's most dangerous enemy, Sir Arthur Wellesley (later the duke of Wellington), paid close attention to infantry firepower. In 1808, for instance, disciplined British troops at Vimeiro in Portugal wrecked the advancing French columns, subjecting Napoleon to his first damaging defeat. The veteran French commander Thomas-Robert Bugeaud de la Piconnerie gave a classic account of what it was like to attack a British position:

> *About a thousand yards from the English line, our men become excited; they start talking and quicken the pace; our column becomes somewhat disordered. The English, firm as a long red wall, are motionless with their arms at the port. . . . They appear to ignore the storm about to break over them, although we are now less than 300 paces from them. This is unnerving. Each of us begins to feel that it will not be pleasant when the enemy, having waited so long, decides to fire. Our ardor begins to cool. We keep up our spirits by shouting all the louder. At last, the English muskets come down—they are making ready. Appalled, many of our men halt and open a scattering fire. Then comes the English volley, precise, deadly, thunderous. Decimated, our column staggers, checks, tries to recover itself. The enemy breaks their long silence with a cheer. Then a second volley, perhaps a third. Then they are upon us, chasing us into disorderly retreat.*

Overextended in Russia and outmaneuvered in Spain, the French hosts retreated to their own homeland. The final reckoning occurred in 1815 at Waterloo, near Brussels, when the repeated attacks of the emperor's army were stubbornly beaten back by the disciplined fire of the British infantry, which was drawn up in unbreachable squares. The fall of men and horses seemed to one British officer "like that of grass before a mower's scythe."

By the end of the day, the two sides had lost a total of more than 50,000 men, and Napoleon's dreams of further conquest had been irreparably shattered. The nationalist fervor that had inspired France would prove to be contagious, however, and in less than a century, it would spur the great powers into the bloodiest and most destructive war of all time.

THE MAKING OF A SOLDIER

"Men are not by nature brave," observed the British field marshal Douglas Haig during the First World War. Yet again and again, the troops of all armies engaged in that war obeyed their officers' commands to rise from the meager shelter of their trenches and advance en masse into a hail of enemy machine-gun fire.

Discipline and unquestioning obedience, even in the face of almost certain death, were recognized as vital elements of success by the earliest military commanders. "Whichever army goes into battle stronger in soul," wrote the Greek soldier and historian Xenophon in the fourth century BC, "their enemies generally cannot withstand them." Some of the ways in which soldiers could be imbued with this strength of soul—which included constant training, the fostering of a heightened sense of loyalty, and systems of reward and punishment—are illustrated on the following pages. The first requirement, however, has always been to get untrained civilians, the raw material out of which all armies are made, off the streets and into the barracks.

In the case of early martial societies such as Greece and Rome, recruitment of an army was not a problem: In return for political rights, all citizens were obliged to perform military service. Under the feudal system of medieval Europe also, landown-ing knights were required not only to don armor in times of war but also to provide foot soldiers from among the serfs who worked their estates. As the feudal system declined during the fifteenth century, commanders relied increasingly on bands of professional soldiers who would fight for any cause provided that the pay was sufficient. But although social elites such as the Junkers of Prussia continued to furnish a ready supply of officers until the end of the nineteenth century, in order to maintain the rank and file of their standing armies, most nations had to rely on either voluntary recruitment or conscription.

The latter method, because of its unpop-

An English propaganda engraving dated 1807 mocks the army of Napoleon Bonaparte by showing conscripts tied together to prevent them from deserting. The English had little cause to feel superior: A pamphleteer in the previous century complained that "officers conduct recruits as prisoners, sometimes marching them pinioned or handcuffed." Fresh recruits were taken quickly to their barracks, or to a port to be dispatched overseas, before they had time to change their minds and make good their escape.

ularity, was often resorted to only in emergencies. During World War I, the British government issued fifty-four million posters and eight million letters to encourage people to volunteer before introducing conscription in 1916. But volunteers were not always preferable to conscripts. Army pay was notoriously low and attracted mainly the desperate: the unemployed, debtors, vagabonds, even petty criminals for whom military service was the only alternative to prison. "The scum of the earth" was the duke of Wellington's blunt assessment of his enlisted men at the beginning of the nineteenth century.

Corruption was rife. The initial bounty payment that served as an incentive for the poor to enlist frequently had to be returned immediately to the army in order to purchase a soldier's basic kit. In seventeenth-century England, many men were tricked into taking the "king's shilling" when they were drunk or when they simply touched a coin that was proffered for inspection. Unscrupulous methods were not exclusive to the government recruiters: In 1787, for example, one Englishman was hanged for making a career out of enlisting—forty-nine times in all—and amassing a fortune in bounty payments in the process. Such incorrigible self-interest was precisely the opposite of what the army needed.

A Roman coin of the second century BC depicts a newly enlisted legionary taking an oath of loyalty. The swearing of allegiance—on a flag, a Bible, the regimental colors, or some other appropriate symbol—has remained in many armies the first step in the transformation from civilian to soldier.

TRAINING AND EQUIPMENT

Specialization came early to war, and with it came the need for more skills than thrusting with sword or spear. Advances in military hardware proved useless unless troops had been trained to realize their benefits: The French discovered during the Franco-Prussian War from 1870 to 1871 that few front-line soldiers knew how to use their new machine gun because its development had been shrouded in secrecy.

Each new weapon also required changes in the tactical deployment of troops, and soldiers had to be trained to perform the maneuvers with the utmost speed. Greek hoplites and Roman legionaries armed with spears and swords were drilled to advance in uniform tight formations; European musketeers and riflemen were taught how to spread out in a line and fire in volleys in response to their officers' curt commands.

Constant rehearsal of procedures was needed to ensure that troops would not be delayed or disoriented by the encumbrance of their equipment or the din and confusion of battle. Habits were so deeply instilled that even when rational thought deserted them, soldiers could, in the words of an American veteran of World War II, "act as automatons, behaving almost as automatically as the machines they operate."

Englishmen hone their skills with bow and arrow in this illustration from a fourteenth-century manuscript. The longbows they are using—which measured up to six and one-half feet—gave greater accuracy and penetrating power than previous bows but demanded more strength and expertise in their firing. At the start of the Hundred Years' War in the mid-fourteenth century, Edward III of England made archery practice compulsory for all yeomen; the result was a series of victories in France won chiefly by the English longbowmen.

German troops mobilizing for the front during the First World War are weighed down by their standard-issue kit, which included flares, rations, water bottles, and other miscellaneous items, as well as rifles and ammunition. The complete pack often weighed almost sixty pounds, and as they stumbled across no man's land toward the enemy trenches, many soldiers threw away nonessential items. An ironic cartoon of the time showed a heavily laden British soldier being asked, "What is a soldier for, Daddy?" "To hang things on, my son."

A nineteenth-century illustration of the Battle of Corinth, fought in 1862 during the American Civil War, shows troops rallying beneath the colors of their respective causes. In battle, uniforms made it instantly apparent which soldiers belonged to which army—here, dark blue for the Union, gray for the Confederate States of America. Until the introduction of olive drab and camouflage in the late nineteenth century, uniforms were often brightly colored to instill pride in their wearers and fear in the enemy.

Forged by their identical uniforms into seemingly unbreakable ranks, Russian military cadets parade through Moscow's Red Square in May 1966. Such precise coordination of movement remained important even after tight infantry formations were no longer used in battle: The sight of men moving in unison could inspire awe in an enemy, and it gave each soldier the confidence of being part of an invulnerable unit.

Depicted on a stone frieze, the battle honors of a Roman legion are carried on conspicuous standards. Such symbolic displays of past victories reinforced the strong identity of each legion—in modern times regimental colors and battle ribbons have fulfilled the same purpose. An enemy's capture of a legion's or regiment's standard—which was the embodiment of its pride—was considered a general dishonor.

ESPRIT DE CORPS

In the heat of battle, a soldier's loyalty needs a more immediate focus than the high ideals that are the staple of politicians' speeches. As the English poet Robert Graves, who served during World War I, wrote: "Patriotism, in the trenches, was too remote a sentiment."

To bridge the gap between ideology and the practical business of fighting, commanders have relied on what one American theorist believed a soldier "holds more dear than life itself: his reputation as a man among men." Most visibly, soldiers are bound to their companions by wearing a standard uniform, and each regiment or similar unit is often distinguished by its own colors and traditions, placing new recruits under an obligation to uphold the honor of their predecessors.

More intimate units engender even stronger ties. Roman legionaries often spent their entire service with the same tentful of colleagues; British troops in World War I frequently served alongside neighbors and friends from their hometowns. Soldiers in such tightly knit groups fought above all for their companions, and knew their compatriots would do likewise.

REWARDS AND PUNISHMENT

ay well, command well, hang well," was a seventeenth-century British general's summary of the art of leadership, emphasizing the carrot of reward and the stick of punishment that were used in all armies to encourage people to fight.

Soldiers' pay has not always been an adequate incentive: A character in Shakespeare's *Pericles* describes war as a condition in which a "man may serve seven years for the loss of a leg, and not have money enough in the end to buy him a wooden one." But before the rise of professional armies, the promise of booty from a sacked city or a share in a prestigious prisoner's ransom was a powerful lure. Since Roman times, more formal systems of reward have included promotion and the awarding of medals for outstanding bravery.

Dread of punishment has proved no less a motivating factor than hope of reward. Desertion and cowardice have long been regarded as capital offenses—the British army did not abolish the death penalty until 1930. The essential principle was defined by Frederick the Great of Prussia in the eighteenth century: "A soldier must fear his own officers more than the enemy."

Troops of the Berliner division are presented the Iron Cross, one of Germany's highest military decorations for bravery, during World War II; the bestowing officer already wears the award pinned to his breast pocket. Such medals have little or no intrinsic worth but are prized by their wearers as the ultimate recognition of their valor. Britain's highest award, the Victoria Cross, was bestowed on only 182 servicemen during World War II.

While drums drown his screams, a British soldier is flogged with a cat-o'-nine-tails in front of his colleagues in this 1844 engraving. Exemplary punishments were frequently meted out for petty offenses. Other penalties included running the gantlet—walking between two ranks of soldiers who lashed the offender as he passed—and, in navies, keelhauling, which involved dragging a sailor by a rope beneath the bottom of his ship.

a daunting objective meant binding the economic and social resources of the North to the war effort to a degree not seen in earlier conflicts. A new stage in the history of warfare was in the making—one in which the entire population of a nation would be directly involved, though not necessarily at mortal risk. That further horror would await the development of large-scale civilian bombing in the twentieth century.

Forty years of relative peace reigned throughout Europe following Napoleon's defeat at Waterloo in 1815. During that long period, the Napoleonic tradition remained paramount in the European armies. Localized conflicts like the Greek War of Independence (1821-1832) did nothing to change the status quo. The generals who led the armies of the major powers remained resolutely backward looking—when a limited war took place between Italy and Austria from 1848 to 1849, the Austrian victory under Field Marshal Joseph Radetzky was firmly rooted in the Napoleonic tradition, using largely Napoleonic weapons.

But already a devastating new infantry weapon was in the making. The first step forward was the replacement of the flintlock by the simpler and more reliable percussion lock. The second was the replacement of the musket by the rifle. Gunsmiths had long known that a rifled gun barrel, by imparting spin to bullets, enormously increased the range and accuracy of a gun. The trouble was loading the bullets, which had hitherto proved so awkward as to rule out the rifle as a practical battlefield weapon. In 1849, however, a French army officer named Captain Claude-Étienne Minié invented a new kind of bullet, which could be loaded as easily into a rifled gun barrel as a round shot could be inserted into a smoothbore and had a range of almost 3,300 feet against the smoothbore's 650.

The early rifles were muzzleloaders, like the smoothbore muskets they replaced. It was a further development of the rifle—the needle gun, so called because of its elongated firing pin—that radically changed the nature of combat. Adopted by the Prussian army in midcentury, the needle gun had twice the range and accuracy of the smoothbore, and five times the rate of fire. At about the same time, the French adopted the chassepot rifle, which could be sighted at about 4,750 feet against the needle gun's 2,450, while the British opted for the Snyder-Enfield, with a rate of fire of six rounds a minute.

The most important specification of these new rifles was that they were breechloading and so could be operated from a prone position, unlike the old muzzleloaders, which required riflemen to stand up to ram the powder and ball down the muzzle. This innovation gave defenders an enormous advantage over attackers—lying flat, they were already well protected even without further fortification. In addition, the firepower generated by the new rifles was so great as to make frontal attacks across open ground virtually suicidal. Even the cavalry could not survive such an assault without suffering unacceptable casualties. Artillery, too, was put at a disadvantage by the breechloading rifle and was forced to unlimber so far from the enemy lines that the effectiveness of its fire was greatly reduced.

To compensate for the artillery's reduced offensive firepower, the French developed the *mitrailleuse,* a primitive kind of machine gun consisting of twenty-five rifle barrels mounted on a gun carriage and firing 150 rounds a minute at a range of just under two miles. A similar weapon, the hand-cranked, water-cooled Gatling gun, firing 200 rounds a minute, was patented in America in 1862 and adopted by the British for many of their colonial adventures. Later in the century came the Maxim

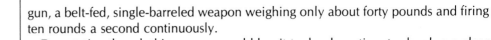

gun, a belt-fed, single-barreled weapon weighing only about forty pounds and firing ten rounds a second continuously.

Devastating though this weapon could be, it took a long time to develop a clear doctrine for its use in the field. Few appreciated the value of very rapid fire, and none foresaw that the machine gun was to become the archetypal weapon of the future, particularly in defense of static lines.

Technological developments beyond the weapons field also did their bit to revolutionize war in the mid-nineteenth century. The steam-powered railroad and the electric telegraph, by facilitating the movement and control of armies, had a profound influence on the outcome of Continental campaigns. All of Europe's major cities were linked by railroad and telegraph by the 1860s. The telegraph could provide speedy communication between commanders and headquarters, while the railroad enabled armies to be transported to the front with unprecedented speed. In the Franco-Austrian conflict of 1859, for example, 600,000 French troops and 129,000 horses were mobilized and carried by train to the front in three months; while in Germany, the railroads were constructed specifically to meet the requirements of the army.

Yet technological progress alone was not enough to transform nineteenth-century armies from essentially Napoleonic entities into modern forces. That required something very rare—a general with a brand-new military mind. Such a man was Count Helmuth von Moltke, who was appointed chief of staff of the Prussian army in 1858 and remained in this post for the next thirty years. A traveler, writer, cartographer, and

In the spring of 1855, toiling British laborers struggle to construct a railroad track in the Crimean port of Balaklava. Amid the bungling chaos of the Crimean War, the railroad that saved front-line troops at Sevastopol a daily trudge of more than five miles to collect supplies shone as a beacon of industrial efficiency. The impact of rail transportation was not restricted to the goods of war, however: In the later nineteenth century, the increased mobility made feasible by the world's ever-growing rail network allowed nations to maintain smaller standing armies and at the same time to expand greatly the possible theater of war.

military intellectual of immense distinction, Moltke was the military genius of his age.

Essentially an innovator and improviser, Moltke methodically set about applying new methods (among them the rifle and the railroad) to the strategies of Napoleonic warfare as interpreted by the German military philosopher Carl von Clausewitz. In the process, he single-handedly created the modern method of directing armies in the field and built up one of the most formidable fighting machines the world had ever seen, the modern Prussian army. For nearly half a century, Moltke's theories and methods were to dominate all military thinking to the extent that the period itself was to become known to military historians as the Age of Moltke.

What made Moltke's contribution to the science of modern warfare original was his wholesale organizational reform of the Prussian army. He increased the authority of the Prussian general staff, dedicated to resolving practical problems of the present, drawing up contingency plans for the future, and disseminating a common doctrine throughout the army. At the same time, he restructured the entire Prussian army. By improving the terms of service, he attracted many more recruits, virtually doubling the size of the army at a stroke. Before long, the Prussians could boast a peacetime army of 180,000 serving on active duty and 355,000 in the reserves—a formidable body of fighting men.

It was the 1853-1856 Crimean War that marked the termination of the period of relative peace that had reigned in Europe since Waterloo. Fought between Russia on the one hand and France, Britain, and Turkey on the other, it was in many ways an old-fashioned conflict—that is, exclusively professional armies met in a limited field of operations under the direction of generals who were brought up in the traditions of the Napoleonic era.

Yet the new age intruded willy-nilly. This was the first war in which rifles and the rifled cannon were used and in which a military railroad was specially built to overcome transportation problems; the first to see an army commander receive directions from his home government by telegraph; and the first to employ such innovative naval weapons as the torpedo, floating mine, and armored warship.

It was also a costly affair, with the Russians losing some 256,000 men and the British and French about 252,000. In spite of the spectacular military casualties suffered in such famous engagements as the Charge of the Light Brigade at Balaklava, however, when the British cavalry suffered 40 percent losses in a brave, magnificent, and utterly stupid attack against the Russian guns, the majority of casualties in the Crimea were the result of diseases like cholera, dysentery, and malaria. It was the pioneer of modern war reporting, William Howard Russell of the London *Times*, who revealed the terrible privations endured by the Allied troops in the Crimea. The general public was outraged, and Florence Nightingale and thirty-eight fellow nurses were dispatched to tend the sick and dying in the British military hospital at Üsküdar. For the first time, perhaps, public opinion at home intruded into military affairs.

Even so, the Crimean War was a far cry from total war, or even from that harbinger of it that broke out in America in 1861. By its end, the American Civil War saw the mobilization of four million men and the complete harnessing of the Union and Confederate economies in support of the respective war efforts. General Ulysses S. Grant, who became overall commander of the Union armies in March 1864, took a brutally simple view of how the war should be fought. "I am determined," he declared, "to hammer continually against the armed forces of the enemy and his resources by sheer attrition, if in no other way, until there should be nothing left for him but submission." Such a war was to cost not only the lives of enemy soldiers but the livelihoods of enemy civilians. Thus the whole population, the entire fabric of society, and its economy were sucked into what started as a purely military conflict.

The American Civil War was a significant war in terms of the huge area across which it was fought (more than 750,000 square miles), the appalling slaughter that ensued from it (more than 620,000 dead, not counting civilian lives, a total greater than the American dead of World War I, World War II, and the Korean and Vietnam wars combined), and its astronomical cost ($2.5 million a day in the North, the economic ruin of the South). More than any other war prior to 1914, the fight to the death between the Union and the Confederacy—between two almost distinct civilizations within one country—conformed to Clausewitz's concept of "the nation at war": a war that demanded the sacrifice of every man, every machine, every dollar for the highest cause.

Never was the strategy of scorched earth employed so ruthlessly in the post-Napoleonic era as it was by the Union side in the American Civil War. It was the brilliant commander of the Union's western armies, General William Tecumseh Sherman, who was to prove the outstanding exponent of this brutal application of total war against the enemy's homeland and civilian population. "We are not only fighting hostile armies but a hostile people," he declared after ordering the expulsion of the entire civilian populace from the occupied rebel city of Atlanta, "and must make young and old, rich and poor, feel the hard hand of war." It was his job to destroy the Southerners' capacity to sustain the conflict by devastating their farms, factories, railroads, and their very will to resist. "We cannot change the hearts of those people of the South," Sherman continued, "but we can make war so terrible and make them so sick of war that generations would pass away before they would again appeal to it."

Sherman's famous march through the South in 1864—his Atlanta campaign—has been described as the greatest feat of arms of the Civil War. It also created an economic desert as his troops systematically destroyed everything in their path on their long, irresistible drive through Georgia and the Carolinas. As one of Sherman's soldiers put it: "We destroyed all we could not eat, stole their niggers, burned their cotton and gins, spilled their sorghum, burned and twisted their railroads, and raised hell generally." This was something new in the annals of modern combat—total war with a vengeance. With their homes burned down, their farms laid waste, and their families starved, the morale of the rebel armies cracked, and they began to melt away—a prelude to the Confederates' looming defeat.

Europe's own descent to Armageddon began with the war between Prussia and Austria in 1866—a conflict deliberately engineered by the Prussians to establish their claim to the leadership of the German Confederation and a future unified Germany. Although the armies of both sides were roughly equal in number, with about 550,000 each, it was generally felt that the Austrians would win because they had recent war experience and the Prussians had not fought a battle for fifty years.

In fact, the reverse proved true. The Prussians were better trained, better organized, and under the sixty-six-year-old Moltke, better led. In addition, their employment of the needle gun gave them a considerable technical advantage. In July 1866, the two armies confronted each other in a crucial battle at Sadowa on the Elbe River. With approximately 250,000 on each side, this was the largest gathering of soldiers since the so-called Battle of the Nations at Leipzig in 1813, and it would not be matched again in scale before World War I. As a consequence of communications problems, one-quarter of the Prussian troops never actually reached the battlefield, but those who did inflicted three times as many casualties on the enemy as they suffered themselves. The Austrian infantry was completely outgunned by the rapid fire of the Prussians' deadly breechloaders. "We have surely done whatever may be expected of brave soldiers," said an Austrian sergeant after the battle, "but no one can stand against that rapid fire."

With Austria defeated, Prussian military might was turned against France. The Franco-Prussian War of 1870 was a trial of strength between the French emperor, Napoleon III, who was committed to a policy of national aggrandizement, and a Prussian chancellor, Otto von Bismarck, no less committed to the unification of Germany under Prussian leadership and the Hohenzollern monarchy.

Moltke's superior planning and transportation network enabled the Prussians to position three entire armies totaling 280,000 men at the front within eighteen days of the opening of hostilities. "The armies that have just taken the field," wrote one military expert at the start of the war, "differ from the armies commanded by Napoleon or the duke of Wellington as much as the latter differed from the Roman legions." Both sides were armed with breechloading rifles and modern field guns, and in the mitrailleuse, the French possessed a weapon that might have won them the war if it had been properly used. So great was the secrecy surrounding the new invention, however, that hardly anyone knew how to work it.

The Germans were not only better organized and better led but superior in both artillery and numbers. In the course of a lightning drive toward Paris—a blitzkrieg of a kind they were to perfect in later wars—the Germans trapped the French army against the Belgian border at Sedan, encircled it, and then destroyed it with shellfire from the surrounding heights. The French lost 17,000 of their troops in the barrage and had no option but to surrender. Of their number, 104,000 were led into captivity—among them, ignominiously, Napoleon III himself and his commander in chief, Marshal Marie-Edme MacMahon.

The Franco-Prussian War not only demonstrated the might and efficiency of a modern army like Moltke's, but the extent to which military violence, or threats of violence, could be used to settle political problems and further the ambitions of aggressive nations. Although forty years of peace were to follow in Europe, it was an uneasy time in which the balance of power was maintained by a complex system of alliances. This was the situation that bred the crisis of 1914.

The general anxiety expressed itself in a seeming paradox. On the one hand, there was an upsurge of antiwar sentiment—the Nobel Peace Prize was first awarded in 1901—and a number of governmental attempts to limit war and reduce armaments, such as the Brussels conference of 1874 and the Hague conference of 1899. On the other, there was an explosion of jingoism and militarism. Numerous patriotic clubs and paramilitary youth movements sprang up, and a multitude of public figures extolled the attraction of war. Among them was the victor of Sedan, Moltke. "Perpetual peace is a dream," he declared. "War is an element of the divine order of the world. In it are developed the noblest virtues of man: courage and self-denial, fidelity to duty, and the spirit of sacrifice. . . . Without war, the world would stagnate and lose itself in materialism."

THE FINAL REPULSE OF THE ZULUS AT GINGHILO

The nineteenth-century European empires helped spread modern warfare and weapons technology to the remotest corners of the globe. By the 1870s, the European powers controlled 67 percent of the world's land surface, and by 1914, the amount had increased to no less than 84 percent. The British were in the forefront of the global takeover. In 1800, they ruled about 1.5 million square miles of the world's surface and 20 million people overseas. During the course of the century, they increased the area of their imperial territory by a factor of seven and the number of their imperial subjects twentyfold; and in the period of time between the Sepoy Rebellion of 1857 and the South African, or Boer, War at the end of the century, they fought more than fifty small wars in a vast area stretching from China to New Zealand and from the Persian Gulf to South Africa.

It was technology that made European expansion possible at a minimum cost in money and lives. The steamboat, for example, greatly facilitated European penetration of Africa and Asia, particularly in its armored form as the naval gunboat—the irresistible symbol of Western power. In the 1830s, the British used gunboats to patrol the Euphrates, Tigris, and Indus rivers, and in China in the 1840s and 1850s, British gunboats decided the outcome of the two Opium Wars.

On land, the new guns enabled European soldiers to overcome native resistance at relatively little cost, spelling an end for traditional native warrior armies. From 1873 to 1874, for example, a British expedition armed with modern rifles, Gatling guns, and field artillery was able to overcome the hugely greater army of the Ashanti, one of the most powerful kingdoms in West Africa.

Imperial forces frequently took a terrible toll of the native armies that stood in opposition to them. And nowhere was the imbalance in firepower more bloodily demonstrated than at Geok-Tepe, in central Asia, where in 1881, a Russian column killed 14,500 tribesmen at a loss of just 59 soldiers. More spectacular still was the carnage inflicted by the British general Lord Horatio Kitchener and his men on the dervish army that was led by religious leader Muhammad Ahmed, called the Mahdi, during the British subjugation of the Sudan. After the critical battle at Omdurman, across the Nile from the Sudanese capital of Khartoum, 10,000 dervishes lay dead, but fewer than 30 Britons.

The litany of imperial bloodbaths carried on into the twentieth century. To establish British influence in Tibet, the British marched in 1904 on the country's capital, Lhasa. On the way, they met the Tibetan army, half of which they slaughtered in the space of a minute or two at a loss of only six wounded. "I was so absolutely sick at that so-called fight," reported the British commander, Colonel Francis Edward Younghusband, "that I was quite out of sorts."

It was only on extremely rare occasions that a native force armed with traditional weapons was capable of defeating a modern European army in pitched battle. One such victory was achieved at Iswandhlwana in 1879, when approximately 20,000 Zulu warriors overwhelmed a British expedition and slaughtered more than 850 British troops and 450 native auxiliaries. The debacle was to be remembered as one of the most spectacular catastrophes in British imperial history.

In this engraving prepared for the *London Illustrated News*, mounted Britons saber their way through Zulu warriors at the Battle of Gingdindlovu in southern Africa; in the background, infantrymen with rifles pick off retreating Zulus with ease. In the late nineteenth century, the superior weapons of European forces enabled them to score easy victories over native armies many times their size in Africa and Asia. These colonial conflicts also offered opportunities for lethal experimentation, notably with the machine gun, which mowed down unprotected enemy troops by the thousands.

The First World War was no misnomer: From corners of the globe as far afield as China, South Africa, Australia, the Middle East, and the West Indies, troops were sucked inexorably into the vortex of European conflict. Most of these foreign contingents came from the colonies of Europe's imperial powers: Those of the British Empire, for example, contributed approximately 2.5 million men.

Some—including more than 1.3 million volunteers from India—enlisted willingly, either from a belief that they were fighting in a just cause or in the hope that their service might be rewarded with independence for their countries. Others, already enlisted in colonial forces, had no choice in their destinies. All, however, were accorded the same shameful treatment. Camps were segregated, racism was rife, pay was low, and discipline was harsh. In addition, only a select few were accorded the dubious honor of service at the front. For the most part, Europe's colonial subjects were seen as a cheap source of mass labor. The background photograph on this page shows members of the Boulogne-based Egyptian Labor Corps, whose work consisted of shifting supplies such as these pyramid-like stockpiles *(inset)*. Those who rebelled against their lot met with merciless retribution: In the closing months of 1917, twenty-three Egyptians and nine Chinese who went on strike at Boulogne were shot.

MUSTERING COLONIAL MANPOWER

On the rare occasions that native armies were able to equip themselves with modern weapons, they had a much greater chance of turning the tables on their European foes. In Algeria and on the North-West Frontier of India, for example, European regulars confronted well-armed adversaries who were able to impose a military stalemate that lasted for decades. Perhaps the most startling achievement of all was the victory won by the Ethiopian ruler Menelik II, who had equipped his army with several thousand of the latest breechloading rifles and a number of machine guns and field guns—in a straight fight at Adwa in 1896, he inflicted a humiliating defeat on an Italian army of 17,000.

For some forty years before the Great War, most of the conflicts involving the European powers—Britain, France, Germany, and Russia—were small-scale colonial ventures, and from their experience in these fields of combat, the generals often drew the wrong conclusions. There was no more striking evidence of their failure than that offered by the British conduct of the South African War between 1899 and 1902—the prolonged and bloody struggle between the British and the Afrikaaners for control of the mainly Afrikaaner Transvaal.

The South African War was not a small war, nor was it colonial in the usual sense, for although the cockpit was indeed a colony, the combatants on both sides were of European origin. The conflict pitted the British regular army against the irregular commando forces of settlers of Dutch stock known as Boers—literally "farmers." It was a singularly bitter struggle, in which the very latest weapons—magazine rifles with smokeless powder, quick-shooting artillery pieces firing shrapnel airbursts— were put to the test.

It was the Boers who started it, by invading British-held territory, and the British who escalated it by dispatching an army double the size of Wellington's at Waterloo. Before the war was over, more than 450,000 British troops had been sent into action against enemy forces totaling roughly one-tenth of that number. Raised in the saddle with gun in hand, the Boers made natural guerrilla fighters, perhaps the best in the world. For the British, they represented a completely new kind of opponent—an army composed entirely of mounted infantrymen who could maneuver on horseback at bewildering speed but could also fight on foot when need dictated. In the multiple skills of horsemanship, marksmanship, and fieldcraft, the Boer volunteers were unsurpassed. They were also armed with up-to-date Mauser repeater rifles, along with some powerful modern artillery.

The British expected the war to be over in three months. Instead, it lasted two and one-half years, and by the end, 22,000 British soldiers had lost their lives, two-thirds of them from disease; a similar number were wounded.

The British had difficulty at first coming to terms with the highly mobile strategy required in a fluid, wide-ranging combat fought over the vast open spaces of South Africa's highveld. Placing too much confidence in their new weapons, they employed the traditional tactic of close-order bayonet attacks against dug-in forces they sometimes could not even see. At Spion Kop, a force of 2,000 men was pinned down and cut to pieces on a bare hill by point-blank rifle fire and an incessant barrage of rapid-firing pompom shells and high explosives. At Magersfontein, an attacking British column was caught by fusillades of rifle fire from the hidden Boer trenches that were so intense it seemed (in the words of a Scottish sergeant) "as if someone had turned on a million electric lights."

Eventually, British firepower told, and the tide of battle turned in their favor. The Boers responded by adopting guerrilla tactics. Only by resorting to a war of attrition were the British able to grind down the obdurate enemy. The Boer homeland was turned into a wasteland. Farms were burned, and more than 150,000 civilians were herded into concentration camps, where many died; of the 24,000 Boers killed in the war, 20,000 were women and children. To secure the land, 8,000 blockhouses were erected across the length and breadth of the old Boer republics, at one-and-one-half-mile intervals.

It was a world of nightmare. On one of Kitchener's security drives against fugitive guerrillas, 9,000 British troops, extended in a line fifty-four miles long, moved forward at a rate of more than eighteen miles a day, while 8,000 more soldiers defended the blockhouses around them. Not until May 1902 did the Boers finally accept British sovereignty, in return for the promise of representative institutions and substantial financial aid to help them rebuild their shattered land.

The last major conflict before World War I started in 1904, with the outbreak of war between Russia and Japan. This conflict was fought on both land and sea and resulted in a decisive victory by an Asian nation over a great European power. It also saw a number of new technological devices brought into play, including the field telephone, the electric searchlight, the giant howitzer, the automatic torpedo, and the anchored mine. Its greatest battle, fought in the Tsushima Strait separating Japan from Korea, was the first to pit ironclad battleships against one another.

Like the Boer War, the Russo-Japanese War was the consequence of an imperial adventure that got out of hand. Extending their empire across northern Asia, the Russians had occupied Manchuria on China's northeastern border, established a powerful Pacific fleet at Vladivostok and Port Arthur (now the Chinese city of

For veteran generals accustomed to combat arenas covering a few square miles, the battlefronts of the First World War, often extending for several hundred miles, presented massive problems of communication. The difficulties had been foreseen by the nineteenth-century German commander Helmuth von Moltke—who initiated the practice of issuing general directives rather than specific commands, thus allowing front-line officers scope for personal initiative in achieving long-term goals—but complex chains of command as well as the sheer numbers of troops involved stretched all communications systems to the limit. Field telephones and telegraphs were of little use: Often the lines were cut by shellfire or, after a successful advance, were simply not there. And when lines did exist, the tapping of Morse-code messages during combat was an impractical and laborious business. Most units fell back on more primitive means of communication such as runners, flares, whistles, and even pigeons.

Portable field telephones such as this German model were often the sole means of communication between isolated detachments of troops.

THE LINES OF COMMAND

Lüshun), and massed an army on the borders of Korea with the aim of extending their grip down to the southernmost tip of the peninsula. But in this aim, the Russians ran up against Japan's own colonial plans, which envisaged Japanese settlement of Korea to create living space for the country's rapidly expanding population.

The signal for the outbreak of hostilities came in February 1904 when Japan launched a surprise attack on the Russian fleet at Port Arthur. Japan's objective was to prevent the Russian navy's interfering with the movement of Japanese troops across the sea to Manchuria and Korea. In this endeavor, Japan was entirely successful, and before long, it had established control over the seaways. Japanese troops quickly overran Korea, invaded Manchuria, and besieged the Russian forces in Port Arthur. It was not until January 1905, however, after a siege lasting nearly a year, that a massive Japanese frontal assault was able to overwhelm the Russian base at a loss of 20,000 Japanese dead.

Two months later, the Japanese won another great and costly victory at Mukden in a prolonged assault against entrenched positions defended by magazine rifles, machine guns, and quick-firing artillery. In the space of four weeks, the Japanese lost 70,000 men and the Russians 100,000 in a bloodbath that anticipated the Armageddon to come. Yet, for all its horrors, Mukden served to confirm the faith of Western military theorists in *l'attaque à l'outrance*—all-out attack, at all times, and at any cost. It was a policy that was to cost them dearly.

Beneath German staff officers who are clustered around a tripod-mounted pair of binoculars, telephone and Morse-code operators issue commands to front-line troops.

The Great War—the first truly global conflict in human history—was now only ten years away. For the preceding half-century, weapons had become deadlier, firepower heavier, armies bigger and better organized, economies richer and more industrialized, nations more ambitious and more overtly jingoistic and bellicose. In spite of its steadily increasing cost in blood and money, war was seen as not only a legitimate but a feasible means of achieving national goals and aspirations, whatever they might be. In addition, the accelerating sophistication of military technology served not so much as a deterrent to war as an apparent guarantee of victory for whoever most successfully deployed it.

New inventions further strengthened the expanding armory. The submarine, the Zeppelin bomber, and the airplane all contained the seeds of revolutionary developments ahead. The Great Powers had in their hands by this time a collection of weapons systems of unparalleled destructive power. During the second decade of the century, they were armed with twentieth-century weapons, which lay at the disposal of political and military leaders possessed of twentieth-century standards of morality but nineteenth-century standards of experience and competence. As a result, statesmen, generals, and whole nations were overwhelmed by the sheer magnitude of the events that were about to unfold. The colossal tragedy of the Great War was to cut deep into the consciousness of modern society and reshape the political order of Europe and, in time, the world.

The war that broke out in August 1914 was not deliberately sought by the Great Powers; instead they were inexorably sucked into it as a consequence of the checkerboard of alliances and interests they had created and the sheer weight of the armies meant to have prevented conflict. Many nations took part, with Britain and the British Empire, France and the French Empire, Italy, Portugal, Greece, Serbia, Romania, Japan, China, and America on the Allied side, and Germany, Austria-Hungary, Bulgaria, and the Ottoman Empire, centered in Turkey, on the other. The war was fought in many theaters. Besides the western and eastern fronts in Europe, there was fighting in Mesopotamia, Persia, and Arabia, in German colonies in East, West, and South-West Africa, and even on the German-held islands of the far-off Pacific. The focal point of the war, however, was Germany. The nation went to war to win a political status commensurate with its newly achieved economic power. The Allies went to war to restrain Germany.

Initially, the war was greeted with enthusiasm in all the major combatant countries. Few among the cheering masses fully understood what was at stake. For many, no doubt, the outbreak of hostilities simply represented an opportunity to escape from routine and boredom. Others saw in the struggle a vehicle for their own youthful idealism—ordeal by battle came to seem a kind of latter-day knightly quest, noble and just, a baptism of fire that was also a form of spiritual regeneration.

"It is like a big picnic," wrote one exhilarated young English officer, Captain Julian Grenfell, in those early days of war rapture. "I have never been so well or happy." Another spoke for many when he declared, "Assuming war had to come, I feel nothing but gratitude to the gods for sending it in my time."

If such reactions to the war were in time to appear naive and unrealistic, they were little more so than the views of the generals who commanded the war-happy volunteers—French, Haig, and Kitchener on the British side; Joffre, Nivelle, Pétain, and Foch on the French; Moltke—a nephew of the victor of the Franco-Prussian War—

Falkenhayn, Hindenburg, and Ludendorff on the German. Few of them had experienced a major war or had ever heard a shot fired in anger. Virtually none of them were able to fathom the nature of the terrible operations they attempted to direct on the battlefields of the western front. When Europe went to war at the beginning of August 1914, no country had made plans for a war lasting more than a few months. "You will be home," the kaiser assured the German army, "before the leaves have fallen from the trees."

He was almost right. In less than three weeks, his troops swept through Belgium and sliced into northern France. By early September, they had reached the Marne River and were threatening Paris. To the west, the Battle of the Marne was followed by a race to the sea in which both sides tried to outflank each other before the Channel ports fell into German hands. Neither won, and the result was a stalemate. Germany remained in control of Belgium and most of northern France but failed to achieve the quick victory the kaiser had promised. Henceforward, his commanders were content to remain on the defensive in the west, dug in behind an impregnable line of trenches that stretched from the Alps to the Channel, while their counterparts on the eastern front dealt with the Russians. For three and one-half years, the Allies were to hurl millions of troops against this line of fortification in a war of attrition, yet at no time before the spring of 1918 was it to vary more than ten miles in depth. "The western front," wrote Robert Graves, "was known among its embittered inhabitants as the 'sausage machine' because it was fed with live men, churned out corpses, and remained firmly screwed in place."

Life in the long, complex warren of almost permanent trenches scooped out of the mud (or, for the lucky ones, chalk) of the fields of France was much the same for all sides—indeed, the opposing trenches were often only a few yards apart. For the greater proportion of the time, there was little action. Boredom, squalor, the miseries of lice, and the form of frostbite known as trench foot, caused by standing for long periods in cold water, were relieved by alcohol, comradeship, and a gallows kind of humor. From time to time, the front-line units were sent back to the rear for a rest. There, the army brothels plied a busy trade. The resulting epidemic of venereal disease was a major drain on personnel. In the British army, for example, there were no fewer than 416,891 cases for the war period.

The dull, comfortless routine of the trenches was punctuated by alarms and high states of readiness, as well as by a variety of hostile missiles that hurtled over sporadically at any time of day and night. It was relatively rarely that the soldiers in any particular sector of the trenches were overwhelmed by the maelstrom of battle.

During the decades that preceded the Great War, the generals and military theorists had debated the problem of how to attack, capture, and hold an enemy's positions. Tactically, this was the crucial operation of war, for without it there could be no territorial gain and no victory, only stalemate. Neither artillery nor cavalry could accomplish this aim on their own, although they could contribute to it. Only the infantry could occupy and hold enemy ground.

The problem was to find a way of doing this against a securely entrenched enemy, armed with modern breechloading rifles and machine guns, that did not involve catastrophic losses. Modern firepower had created an impasse. The only answer, the generals decided, was to use the artillery to blast a way through for the infantry. "Breaking through the lines is largely a question of expenditure of high explosive ammunition," declared General Sir John French, the commander in chief of the

GOING TO GROUND IN THE TRENCHES

It is a nasty, wet, chalky dugout full of rats and creeping things." The conditions so described by a British soldier in 1916 were endured by both Allied and German troops during World War I along a front that stretched for more than 460 miles between Switzerland's border and the North Sea. The primitive and unsanitary dugouts, trenches, and underground bunkers had become the characteristic fortifications of modern warfare.

Originally used by besieging armies to provide protection for advancing troops, trenches were first widely employed in the American Civil War, when generals on both sides realized that riflemen sheltered in dugouts could be dislodged only at a great cost in casualties to the attacking force. During the First World War, the lesson was taken to its logical conclusion: Entire armies entrenched in the earth faced each other across a no man's land that was often less than 150 feet wide.

Behind the front trench on each side, a maze of communications led back to headquarters and supply depots. Every trench was dug in a crooked rather than a straight line—to minimize the damage caused by exploding shells and to prevent the enemy from obtaining a direct line of fire along an entire trench. Constant maintenance was necessary to shore up trench walls, to bail out floodwater, and to repair gaps in the outer defenses of barbed wire. For the human occupants of the trenches—mired in mud, infested with lice, freezing in winter, and sweltering in summer—war could hardly have been less glorious.

Union soldiers relax among the dugouts and trenches of a captured Confederate stronghold outside Atlanta during the American Civil War.

During a lull in hostilities in the First World War, exhausted British soldiers huddle in the shelter of a trench wall.

British Expeditionary Force on the western front in January 1915. "If sufficient ammunition is forthcoming, a way out can be blasted through the line."

Heavy artillery thus became the dominant offensive weapon of the Great War, just as the machine gun became the dominant defensive weapon. The statistics are awesome. In the Russo-Japanese War, artillery inflicted 10 percent of the casualties; in the Great War, the figure was 70 percent. In some set-piece engagements, the sheer weight of artillery fire was extraordinary. At the battles of Arras and Vimy Ridge in April 1917, for example, British artillery fired almost 2.7 million shells from guns positioned at twenty-six-foot intervals along an eleven-mile front. At the beginning of the Third Battle of Ypres in June, the British fired 3 million shells in a barrage that lasted seven days, and in the following month, as the offensive entered its main phase, they fired another 4 million shells—an entire year's production, brought up in

Belying its nickname, the "land battleship," a British tank lies stranded in the waterlogged terrain of Ypres in 1917. Introduced by the British on the Somme in 1916, tanks were first employed en masse the following year at the Battle of Cambrai, where they enabled British troops to advance with far fewer casualties than had become the norm. They were armed with light cannon or machine guns, and despite their sluggish average speed of five miles per hour, they possessed the vital mobility that allowed troops to follow up an attack successfully. The Germans, who were slow to perceive the tactical potential of the tank, did not bring their own version into service until March 1918.

320 trains—from guns positioned every sixteen feet along the front. But all the effort was in vain. Time and again, it was shown that artillery alone, no matter how heavy, could not eliminate a well-entrenched defense.

Under the artillery's rain of death, the foot soldiers launched their assaults. Often the advance had to be made across terrain stripped bare of tree cover by incessant shellfire and obstructed by a myriad of waterlogged shell craters. Usually, a hail of fire greeted the attacking formations as they came forward, with bayonets fixed, across the no man's land that separated the two sets of trenches.

By far, the most lethal component of the enemy fire came from the machine guns, which were organized in pairs or in batteries of four to eight guns in order to create an extensive field of fire. With a range of about 8,200 feet, an extremely rapid rate of fire, tremendous stopping power, and fixed elevation, the guns could systematically traverse lines of oncoming infantry troops with long sweeps of continuous fire. The result was carnage. Whole waves of soldiers were scythed down and lay in long rows where they had fallen. To make matters worse, the defenders could bring their own artillery to bear on the attacking infantry with a counterbarrage of airburst shrapnel shells that would inflict further casualties.

Even if the assault gathered sufficient momentum to carry some troops through to the enemy's outer defenses, they could find themselves ensnared by a barbed-wire perimeter about thirty-three feet wide, where riflemen in the trenches could easily pick them off. And if they survived that hazard, the ultimate horror of close, hand-to-hand combat remained. The close-quarter combat that took place in the trenches was brief, wild, and terrible because it was so personal and so primitive. As an Australian infantryman put it: "Bayonet fighting is indescribable—a man's emotions race at feverish speed, and afterward, words are incapable of describing feelings." A German corporal, Stephan Westman, ordered to attack French positions in 1915, described a typical incident:

> During the ensuing melee, a French corporal suddenly stood before me, both our bayonets at the ready, he to kill me, I to kill him. . . . Pushing his weapon aside, I stabbed him through the chest. He dropped his rifle and fell, and the blood shot out of his mouth. I stood over him for a few seconds, and then I gave him the coup de grâce. After we had taken the enemy position, I felt giddy, my knees shook, and I was actually sick.

Persuading men repeatedly to expose themselves to such conditions was a problem to which the generals gave much thought. In every attack, there would come a point when the attacking infantry had to move out of the cover of supporting fire and into the so-called zone of death. It was found that troops were much more likely to keep going forward at this crucial juncture when they did so in close proximity to their comrades—comradeship and solidarity gave them cohesion and confidence under the extreme stress of fire. Indeed, the French high command recommended that the infantry should advance to the attack "elbow to elbow in mass formations, to the sound of bugles and drums."

The soldiers of the western front, then, were condemned to march into the zone of death in mass formations. Only in this way, it was believed, could they be persuaded to advance at all. The really important element in modern warfare, it was argued, was not material technology but human morale—the inculcation of the desire to win and the spirit of self-sacrifice. "War," wrote one of Britain's more astute Great War commanders, General Sir Ian Hamilton, "is essentially the triumph, not of a chassepot over a needle gun . . . but of one will over a weaker will."

From that viewpoint, it followed that great losses had to be accepted as a test of the will power necessary to achieve victory. As one military theorist declared: "The true strength of an army lies essentially in the power of each or any of its constituent fractions to stand up to punishment, even to the verge of annihilation if necessary." The appalling casualties that ensued were seen not as the result of military incompetence but as a measure of national resolve.

In practice, however, will power was not always enough, and various devices had to be used to persuade soldiers to go over the top while under fire. Alcohol was one. In the British army, a large tot of rum was ladled out to each man immediately before an assault was launched. A German soldier recalled how his comrades grew desperate for a drink during heavy bombardments. "They have a craving for brandy that can hardly be satisfied," he reported, "which shows how badly they yearn to lose the faculty of feeling."

Sometimes an appeal was made to the men's sporting instincts. As the whistle blew for the British attack on the Somme on July 1, 1916, for example, one company commander in the East Surrey Regiment kicked a soccer ball long and high toward the German line and then charged after it into no man's land, pursued by all his troops. He provided balls for each of the four platoons under his command and offered a prize for the first person to dribble a ball through the German defenses. No one ever collected the prize, however, for the officer was killed in the attack, along with a large number of his men.

Many soldiers sought comfort in superstition and magic. No soldier was without his charm or lucky coin. Sometimes a supernatural force was believed to extend a collective protection, like the famous Angel of Mons, a cloudy apparition said to have appeared in the sky above British troops retreating from the Belgian town of Mons in August 1914, keeping them from harm. The spiritual comfort of conventional religion, too, was readily available, and chaplains on both sides were often at the front to say Mass, distribute Holy Communion, or give absolution to the dying. As the Americans used to say, you never found an atheist in a foxhole.

All the combatants, naturally, believed that God was on their side. As the English poet and humorist J. C. Squire commented:

> God heard the embattled nations sing and shout:
> "Gott straffe England"—"God save the King"—
> "God this"—"God that"—and "God the other thing":
> "My God," said God, "I've got my work cut out."

For many front-line soldiers, fear of appearing a coward was the stick that drove them across the killing fields. As one young English infantry captain wrote home before his first attack in January 1917: "The only thing I'm not certain about is whether I may get the wind up and show it. I'm afraid of being afraid." But there were also more practical reasons for apprehension. Anyone who failed to go over the top when ordered to do so faced rough justice by court-martial or could even be summarily executed on the spot by a superior officer or the military police.

Even so, there were times when some men reached the limit of their endurance. Between April and June 1917, for example, there were 250 mutinies in sixty-eight divisions of the French army. Pushed beyond the breaking point by a series of disastrous attacks against heavily fortified positions in the Champagne region, the troops simply refused to obey orders, and many thousands deserted. In retribution, the army was punished by the procedure known as decimation—every tenth man was hauled off and charged. More than 100,000 soldiers were court-martialed, of whom 23,000 were found guilty, 432 sentenced to death, and 55 officially shot (although more were shot without being sentenced). Another 250 were allegedly placed in front of their own artillery and pounded to death by shellfire. Nevertheless, the mutineers won their main point—no more futile offensives were ordered.

For the most part, however, the troops on both sides accepted their lot with weary resignation. Few major battles were fought without tremendous casualties, but none were so great as those suffered in the Somme offensive of 1916. In the southern sector, the attack made substantial progress, but in the north, it was a costly failure. Whole battalions were virtually wiped out. Out of 800 men of the 10th Yorkshire and Lancashire Regiment, for example, only 40 were left. The First Newfoundland Regiment lost 658 men and every officer in forty minutes, cut down in rows by concentrated machine-gun fire. By noon, the bodies of nearly 50,000 dead or wounded British infantrymen littered the half-mile or so of open ground in no man's land. By nightfall, the final toll had reached 21,000 dead and 35,000 wounded, with 600 men taken prisoners of war. One division, the 34th, had lost nearly 75 percent of its infantry between sunrise and sunset.

With the coming of dark, no man's land came alive with shuffling noises as wounded men tried to crawl back to their own lines. Some were screaming, others demented with shock. Ten thousand of the wounded were still lying helpless on the battlefield without medical aid the next day. Many of them drowned as heavy rain slowly filled up the shell holes in which they had sought refuge. Some survivors were trapped in no man's land for days—two were not found until fourteen days after the attack, having survived on water from the bottom of a crater.

Wearing gas masks, British soldiers crouch at the ready behind their Vickers machine gun. Beneath the barrages of screaming artillery shells, trench fighting had a primitive quality epitomized by the equipment shown at left: a British Mills bomb, a chemically impregnated flannel hood to protect against gas, a wooden truncheon studded with hobnails, and a German stick grenade. Each soldier favored his own ad hoc weapon—a knobkerrie cudgel or a tin can packed with explosive—but it was the face-splitting potency of a sharpened entrenching tool that held the most universal appeal.

Belching smoke, a German "Long Max" gun sends a shell flying toward the French capital from its fifty-six-foot-long barrel. From its wooded lair near Crépy, about seventy miles distant, the Long Max was able to bombard Paris with impunity. The massive shells (above) each weighed almost 200 pounds; they could be loaded and fired by the gun's sixty-man crew at a rate of one every fifteen minutes. During the five months following its introduction in March 1918, the Long Max fired more than 452 shells into Paris, one of which landed on a church, killing a Good Friday congregation of eighty-eight people. Despite its range and the mobility afforded by its railroad undercarriage, however, the Long Max had more effect on Allied morale than on the actual outcome of the war.

The casualty figures from the first day of the Somme easily exceeded the number lost at the Battle of Waterloo a century earlier—the previous British record for a single day's fighting. They even surpassed by a wide margin the British battle casualties of the Crimean War and Boer War combined. By the end of the Somme offensive in November, British casualties had risen to 420,000, and the final casualty figure for both sides came to the lunatic total of 1,070,000.

Confronted with an endlessly bloody impasse on the western front, the generals looked for alternative ways of dealing the enemy a fatal blow. For a while, it looked as though poison gas might do the trick. The Germans were the first to use it, experimenting initially with chlorine gas, then switching to mustard gas, which was borne by the wind over the enemy trenches. The new weapon caused panic and dread, along with horrific injuries: At Ypres in April 1915, it blew an almost four-mile gap in the British line. But protective measures were soon devised that largely neutralized its effectiveness.

Other efforts to break the deadlock entailed opening costly sideshows in other theaters of combat. One such was the Gallipoli campaign, fought on a peninsula of Turkey at the end of the Dardanelles. There, an Allied attempt to open a route to Constantinople and knock Turkey out of the war by a bold amphibious action ground to a halt and ended with an ignominious withdrawal and 200,000 British, French, Australian, and New Zealand casualties. (Anzac—Australian and New Zealand Army Corps—losses in the Great War reached 62 percent of all those who served, the highest of all units from the Anglo-Saxon world.)

More than one million British and empire troops were subsequently tied up in a two-pronged campaign against the southern flanks of Turkey's Ottoman Empire, with 600,000 in Mesopotamia for the march on Baghdad, and another 500,000 troops in Palestine for the march on Jerusalem and Damascus. These campaigns achieved their objectives, preventing the Turks from providing any real support to the Germans in the West and eventually bringing about the downfall of the Ottoman Empire. But they did little to change the course of events on the battlefields of Europe. The stalemate between the Germans and the Western Allies remained.

New weapons appeared to offer one possible route out of the deadlock. On the German side, it was believed that the stalemate on land could be solved by a breakthrough in the air. For only Germany had the giant, rigid airships popularly known as Zeppelins after their inventor; and at the beginning of the war, the dirigibles were the only kind of aircraft that possessed the range and capacity to carry substantial bombloads over enemy terrain and thus pursue a strategic air campaign against targets on the ground.

Both the army and navy possessed airship divisions. The extent of their operations was remarkable. Army airships, for example, launched raids against an extraordinary number of the great cities of Europe, including Paris, London, Bucharest, Riga, Minsk, Brest Litovsk, Odessa, Sevastopol, Naples, Brindisi, and Salonika, as well as the Ploieşti oil fields of Romania and the Aegean Islands of Greece. The naval craft, under their redoubtable chief Captain Peter Strasser, pursued a systematic campaign against Britain. Strasser had a passionate faith in the Zeppelins, believing they could bring the war to a speedy conclusion by paralyzing Britain's industry and demoralizing its people. In a series of fifty-one raids, the Zeppelins dropped more than 200 tons of bombs on British targets from the English Channel to the lowlands of Scotland.

The greatest single incident took place in September 1916 when sixteen giant airships, each the size of an ocean liner and inflated with inflammable gas, set off in a spectacular attempt to deliver a knockout blow to the British capital. But waiting for them now were high-flying fighter planes that were equipped with incendiary bullets—the Zeppelins' size made them easy targets, and the hydrogen that kept them airborne caught fire easily.

By the end of their campaign, the Zeppelins had killed 557 Britons and done substantial damage to property. But their attacks were never more than a pinprick against the British war effort. Indirectly, however, the raids contributed to the increasing war-weariness of the British populace; they also tied up troops and planes that might otherwise have been used on the battlefield. But the cost was high. Approximately 40 percent of the navy airship crews were killed, and fifty-three of seventy-three airships were destroyed.

In 1917, twin-engined Gotha aircraft took over the German strategic bombing role, making several successful daylight raids on London and inflicting substantial damage. In retaliation, the British planned to escalate the air war with raids over Berlin using Handley-Page heavy bombers. But the war ended before the raids could be launched. At the end, the strategic bombing war turned out to be more a presage of things to come than an effective means of changing the course of the war. But the military aircraft was clearly established as a new and potentially devastating weapon.

A more profound effect on the conduct of the war was exercised by the German *Unterseeboot,* or U-boat. The submarine blockade of British waters was Germany's answer to the naval blockade of Germany imposed by Britain. Britain's weakness was that it was dependent on sea communications for all of its oil, much of its food, and most of the raw materials necessary for the war effort. By destroying Britain's sea links, it was argued, the nation could be brought to its knees.

As early as February 1915, when hope for a quick victory in the land war had faded, the Germans launched an unrestricted submarine campaign around the coast of Britain directed against all shipping, including neutral boats, entering the war zone. By 1917, the U-boats were close to achieving their aim. In April of that year, the peak month of the campaign, German submarines sank about 950,000 tons of shipping, causing Britain's Admiralty to forecast that if losses continued at that rate, the war would be lost by November. In fact, Britain found an answer to the threat in the escorted convoy system, which by November had reduced U-boat sinkings to a more tolerable 285,000 tons. At the same time, immense mine barriers containing a total of 165,000 devices were laid across the U-boat lanes in the English Channel and the North Sea, cutting off the boats from their bases, and depth charges and Allied air cover made life increasingly perilous for the submarine crews.

Britain narrowly survived the U-boat threat. In all, the submarines sank nearly 5,000 ships totaling about 12 million tons, and most of those were British. But their own losses were also great: More than half their boats and 40 percent of their crews went down. In addition, the extension of the U-boat blockade to American waters, and the deaths of American citizens in some of the ships they torpedoed, were to play a major part in bringing the United States into the war on the side of the Allies.

In both Britain and Germany, where there were no foreign armies fighting on native soil, a great gulf of incomprehension gradually split the civilians at home from the fighting men at the front. Noncombatants could not begin to understand what the

In a futile attempt to achieve a breakthrough on the Somme, British troops rise from their trenches and proceed toward the enemy on September 25, 1916. Despite the prodigious killing power of modern armaments, it was widely believed by military leaders that enemy positions could be taken only by solid waves of advancing soldiers. The result was a tide of humanity that ebbed and flowed between opposing trenches at horrific cost and to little advantage. According to one soldier's account, "the attacks assumed a drearily stereo-typed pattern" that concluded with "three-quarters to nine-tenths dead, or dying with their bowels hooked on the wire of no man's land . . . hoping only to attract the merciful attention of an enemy machine gunner."

troops on the western front were going through, while the soldiers themselves, when they went home on leave, tended to become contemptuous of the naive and jingoistic attitudes of the people around them and envious of their comfort and complacency.

Yet even on the home front, attitudes began to change as the casualty lists grew longer, and the names of relatives and friends began to appear on them with increasing frequency. And some civilians found themselves sucked into the war in earnest—all over Europe, refugees were forced to flee the fighting. One hundred thousand Belgian civilians sought refuge in Britain after their country was occupied by the German army. In eastern Europe, whole villages were uprooted or destroyed in an all-embracing war of movement. Hunger was also an enemy. As the British naval blockade of Germany began to tighten, the German populace went hungry, and in the hard winter of 1916 to 1917, turnips formed the staple diet. The U-boat blockade of Britain threatened to have a similar impact, and by late 1917, the nation's stock of wheat was down to one month's supply.

By now, the struggle had become total in both Britain and Germany: The war economy subjugated all the vital activities of the nation to the overriding needs of the military. In Britain, for example, state direction of labor and central control of shipping and agriculture were introduced. From the beginning of 1916, there was compulsory conscription of men, and increasingly (in a social shift of almost revolutionary proportions), it was women who made up the work force of the nation. With the entire resources of the country harnessed to servicing the war machine, arms manufacturing became an even more profitable industry, especially for the makers of shells, for which there was an insatiable appetite at the front. As the conflict bogged down in a prolonged war of attrition and hope of an early victory receded, the bellicose euphoria of the opening phase began to give way to exhaustion and war-weariness, a longing to get it over.

Events refused to oblige. By 1917, the war was still in a state of deadlock. The Germans had thrown back the Allies' big spring offensive on the western front, in spite of British and Canadian successes at Arras and Vimy Ridge, won at huge cost—150,000 British and Canadian casualties, 100,000 German. A shift in the balance of the war looked likely when the United States declared war on Germany in April, although the advantage was partly canceled out when Russia began to pull out of the war a few months later, leaving Germany a freer hand in the West. All sides increasingly doubted whether victory was possible. Everywhere, the war was deeply unpopular with the people at large.

The generals remained unmoved by the spreading doubts and dismay. In another attempt to break the deadlock, the British commander in chief, Douglas Haig, launched a frontal assault at Ypres, which had been the scene of two previous battles. As a preliminary measure, he had the German positions mined with an explosive charge so enormous that when it went off, the sound could be heard in the prime minister's room at 10 Downing Street in London, more than 124 miles away across the English Channel. Then he sent hundreds of thousands of his troops into the treacly mud of no man's land and the ghastly slaughter around the small Belgian town of Passchendaele. In this, the last, disastrous, old-style battle of the war, 300,000 British troops and 200,000 Germans were killed or wounded. The gains were minimal.

The year 1918 seemed to promise the same bloody stalemate as before. But the overall situation had changed. One-half of the war in Europe came to an end in

Packed in coffins in a shallow grave, bodies from the doomed British ocean liner *Lusitania* await mass burial. Ostensibly carrying only passengers, the *Lusitania* was in fact also laden with American arms and ammunition destined for Britain when it was torpedoed off southern Ireland on May 7, 1915, by a German submarine—as pictured in a German postcard *(inset)*. The death of nearly 1,200 civilians, among them 128 American citizens, caused international outrage, and two years later, the United States entered the war on the side of Britain and France. By this time, all parties had digested the lessons taught by the *Lusitania*'s sinking: that submarines were a significant addition to the arsenal of modern warfare, and that in the era of total war, civilians were no less at risk than soldiers.

March, when Russia's new Bolshevik rulers made peace with the Germans at Brest Litovsk, bringing to an end the fighting on the eastern front. But by now, Germany was in a desperate plight. Its allies were weakening or wavering, and the British blockade was causing severe shortages and even hunger at home. With American troops pouring into the western front, the German generals realized that they had but one last chance to win victory.

On March 21, 1918, under cover of fog and with no preliminary bombardment, the Germans overran the British positions south of Saint-Quentin on the Somme in a lightning thrust toward the Channel ports, and in the following week, they advanced farther than they had ever advanced before. For the first time since the autumn of 1914, the war in the West became a war of movement—the only kind of war in which a victory could be won.

In a renewed offensive in July, the Germans broke through to the Marne and advanced to within fifty-six miles of Paris. But three weeks later, the British counterattacked, deploying a weapon that at last had the potential to break the bloody stalemate of the trenches. On August 8, 1918, an armada of 456 tanks, with infantry and cavalry support, growled toward the German defensive line in an advance that finally destroyed the Germans' will to win. On September 26, 1918, the Allies launched the final offensive of the war. Although they failed to break through or encircle the German positions, and the Americans suffered 100,000 casualties in the course of an eight-mile advance, Germany's chief of staff, General Erich von Ludendorff, was adamant that there should be an immediate armistice.

It was not simply the danger threatened by the Allied push to his front that persuaded the general, but the collapse of Germany's allies to the rear. The Ottoman Empire had dissolved, with the Allies at the gates of Constantinople and the British advancing on the oil fields of Mesopotamia. The Hapsburg empire of Austria-Hungary had also collapsed and was in the process of fragmenting into the independent states of Poland, Czechoslovakia, Hungary, Romania, and Yugoslavia. Germany's back door was wide open, and the Allies were planning to burst through from the south. The High Seas Fleet had mutinied, and the country was on the verge of revolution. There seemed no alternative but to sign the piece of paper that represented Germany's defeat.

At 10 a.m. on November 11, 1918, the British reentered the historic city of Mons and thus returned to the place from which they had started at the very beginning of the war. An hour later—the eleventh hour of the eleventh day of the eleventh month of the year—the guns finally fell silent, and a miraculous and deathly hush descended on the western front.

In the streets of London that evening, the crowds sang and danced, and in the euphoria of victory, complete strangers were said to have copulated in public. But for the soldiers who had survived the slaughter, relief was counterpointed with exhaustion and with mourning for their fallen comrades.

More than 70 million men had been mobilized to fight in the Great War. Nearly 9 million—one in eight—had died. These were the men of the Lost Generation. Nearly all had been under thirty years of age, and most had been civilians in uniform—agricultural laborers on the Continent, industrial workers in England and Scotland. The Germans suffered grievous losses, with up to 2 million dead. The French lost 1.3 million of their young men, the British Empire nearly a million, including .75 million from Britain alone. Yet the body counts on the western front

IN
EVERLASTING
MEMORY
OF THE MEN OF
MINEHEAD
WHO LAID DOWN
THEIR LIVES IN THE
GREAT WAR
1914-1918.

C. PRESCOTT	H. STEPHENS
H. PUGSLEY	C. J. SWEETLAND
E. J. QUANTICK	C. H. THOMAS
A. A. QUICK	F. C. TUDBALL
F. RAWLE	A. M. TUDBALL
J. W. REDD	H. WARRE
F. REED	F. J. WEBBER
C. F. J. RICHARDSON	H. J. WEBBER
W. H. SHERRIFF	L. WEBBER
G. H. SLADE	S. C. WEBBER
T. C. SLADE	W. J. WEBBER
T. SLADE	T. WESCOMBE
H. SMITH	C. J. WILLIAMS
Hy. SMITH	H. WILLIAMS
W. W. SPARKES	F. WILLIS
J. STARK	G. W. WYATT

were outdone by those in the East. The Russians suffered the greatest overall losses, with more than 2 million dead, while Serbians, Romanians, Bulgarians, and Turks suffered the greatest losses in proportion to the size of their populations. The Americans, who came late into the fighting, suffered 115,000 dead.

The total of military casualties, including wounded, prisoners, and missing, was about 37.5 million—more than 22 million on the Allies' side, 15 million for the Central Powers. A statistical analysis of British casualties showed that shells and mortar bombs caused 58 percent of casualties, bullets 39 percent, grenades just over 2 percent, and bayonets 0.32 percent. Perhaps it is not surprising that the most decorated British soldier of the Great War—Private W. H. Colman VC, DCM and Bar, MM—was a stretcher-bearer. In addition, between 9 million and 12.6 million civilians were estimated to have died as a result of the war.

It was clear that Europe would never be the same again. The First World War had seared the collective psyche of the Continent. The great dynasties of the Hohenzollerns, the Hapsburgs, the Romanovs, and the Ottomans had been destroyed; their departure was a portent of sweeping, even revolutionary, changes to come. The reverberations of the conflict were to be felt throughout the world in the ensuing decades. So terrible had been the cost that people sought solace in the assertion that this had been "the war to end war."

Others had their doubts. German troops—among them a skinny Austrian corporal with a First Class Iron Cross named Adolf Hitler—had returned from the front resentful, defiant, proud, and professional, convinced they had been stabbed in the back, defeated not by the enemy but by moral collapse at home. The punitive peace terms imposed on the German nation by the victorious Allies at Versailles in 1919 proved more likely to inflame the German problem than assuage it. A few perceptive observers saw that for many Germans, the Great War was unfinished business. In 1920, a British journalist named Charles A'Court Repington published his war diaries. In them, he coined for the first time a pessimistic new name for the conflict—the "First World War." The Great War indeed marked the end of an era—but it was also to serve as a prelude to a second and even more awful holocaust.

SUSTAINING AN ARMY

Sergeant Edward Costello, in his memoirs of the Peninsula War from 1808 to 1814, recorded that for days on end, the common experience of his companions was "cold, hunger, and fatigue," and that often their sufferings "were such that many of them considered death a happy release." Roman soldiers campaigning in northern Europe in the first century BC would have recognized this complaint; so would American troops in Vietnam in the 1970s. And generals throughout history have known that to sustain the morale of their armies, the rigors of campaign life must be alleviated—by the provision of adequate shelter, food, medical care, and off-duty activities.

Some of the ways in which armies have catered to these needs are illustrated on the following pages. The ablest military administrators have devoted no less time and energy to support facilities than have generals to battle tactics. The Ottoman sorties into central Europe in the sixteenth century, for example, were meticulously organized to take full advantage of the short campaigning season before bad weather set in: Months in advance, orders were sent out to foundries for gun carriages and other vital equipment; roads were kept in good repair; and the army was accompanied by herds of sheep and cattle for fresh meat, as well as

by numerous bakers, butchers, saddlers, and smiths. The wagon shown above in the tapestry detail, part of the baggage train attached to the duke of Marlborough's army in France in 1708, was specifically designed to cope with the rough and muddy roads of Europe in winter.

Even the most thorough commanders cannot eliminate all hardships. But a measure of hunger, pain, and boredom has always been accepted by most soldiers as no less a part of their lot than combat. Edward Costello, after he had safely returned to England in 1814, noted that "our men soon forgot the fatigues of the peninsula campaigns; and being joined by a batch of recruits and supplied with new clothing, the old soldiers once more panted for fresh exploits; for their souls were strong for war, and peace became irksome to them."

Australian officers kill time in their dugout during the Battle of Ypres in 1917. Troops in World War I generally spent only two out of every four weeks in the front-line trenches; idle hours were occupied by writing letters home, delousing, and mending uniforms and equipment.

A 1598 German illustration shows a military camp that is virtually a township: Within a horseshoe-shape barrier of wagons are tents—well-appointed for officers, basic for troopers—shops, animals, cooking fires, and in the center, a gallows to enforce discipline.

Life in the field is probably the feature of war that has changed least over the centuries. Roman legionaries slept in leather tents roomy enough for ten men; troops in the 1991 Persian Gulf War bedded down under canvas. But the simplicity of the tent contrasts with the complex arrangements needed for the encampment of an army on the move: After a day's march burdened with equipment, chores include gathering fuel for cooking fires, digging latrines, and erecting perimeter defenses. Troops defending a fixed frontier have time to build bunkers or other less temporary shelters, but the business of keeping the soldiers well-supplied and alert is no less demanding. As armies became larger and their weapons more sophisticated, their backup needs proliferated. During the Vietnam War, for example, service and support units accounted for about three-quarters of all American personnel.

The observation that "an army marches on its stomach," attributed to Napoleon, was no new discovery. Roman legionaries engaged in campaigns carried three days' rations with them—chiefly grain, which was ground and then baked into hard biscuits—and the granaries in their fortresses were constantly replenished. In Europe during the seventeenth century, a soldier's daily rations, according to one officer, might include two pounds each of bread and meat and one bottle of wine or two of beer. But the numbers of soldiers and pack animals often far exceeded the available supplies, and most armies on lengthy campaigns resorted to plundering the surrounding countryside. Not until the invention of canning in the nineteenth century was the quartermasters' task eased: canned meat, according to the British soldier T. E. Lawrence, "modified land warfare more profoundly than the invention of gunpowder."

A stylized depiction of a camp on an Assyrian stone relief from the ninth century BC shows cooks fanning grilled food and stoking a fire beneath a cauldron. In the lower left quadrant, a priest examines the entrails of a slaughtered animal, possibly to foretell the outcome of a coming battle.

A German engraving of 1812 shows troops returning to their camp with stolen goats and poultry. Because such brigandage embittered local populations, many commanders—including those of the Ottoman army in the sixteenth century and Mao Zedong during the Chinese civil war in the 1940s—insisted that their troops pay for all food taken from farms and villages.

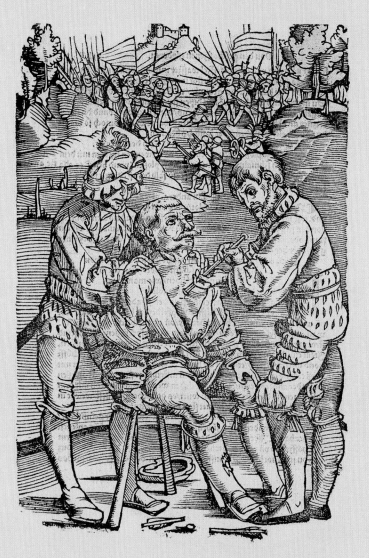

In an engraving from a sixteenth-century German manual of field surgery, an arrow is removed from a soldier's chest. Prior to the discovery of anesthetics, a soldier might be dulled with opiates or alcohol—or have a limb numbed by a tight tourniquet—before the surgeon applied the scalpel.

A stretcher-borne casualty is gently maneuvered from a French ambulance train in 1915. Soldiers who required immediate surgery were dealt with in stations behind the front lines; others were transported to base hospitals, some of which had 20,000 beds.

In a third-century-BC contract of service offered to Greek mercenaries, adequate medical care was one of the principal terms. But for centuries, the treatment of the maimed and the sick was bedeviled by ignorance: Often those who died of their wounds were far fewer than those who died of subsequent infection or of diseases unfamiliar to their doctors. The importance of cleanliness and nutrition was clearly demonstrated during the Crimean War in 1854, when in the stinking warren that was the British field hospital, Florence Nightingale and her thirty-eight nurses reduced the death rate of those admitted from nearly 50 percent to less than 3 percent. The founding of the Red Cross in 1864 and the introduction of disinfectants and of anesthetics before surgery greatly improved the survival chances of the wounded.

GUARD AGAINST

VD
VENEREAL DISEASE

KEEP STRAIGHT KEEP SOBER

YOU OWE IT TO YOURSELF · YOUR WOMENFOLK
YOUR COMRADES · YOUR COUNTRY

A British poster from
World War II warns sol-
diers to protect themselves
against venereal disease.
Of more practical use was
the distribution of con-
doms, initiated during
World War I.

A German engraving dated
1598 shows a procurer
urging newly recruited
prostitutes toward a military camp. In India during
the nineteenth century,
the British established regimental brothels, where
the women had regular
medical examinations.

Marilyn Monroe delights
an audience of more than
10,000 U.S. troops during
the Korean War. During
World War II and later
conflicts, many Western
nations organized tours of
base camps abroad by
popular entertainers.

To make up for the lack of female com-
panionship, soldiers have generally had to
rely on their own initiative. Many men stationed in garrison towns took up with local
women: "I know one woman personally
who was the wife of three husbands in six
months," recalled a British sergeant in India in the 1840s, despite the fact that "soldiers in general make such bad husbands."

Modern armies have made more formal arrangements for the relaxation of their soldiers: The facilities provided for American
troops in Vietnam, for example, included
sports, movies, and drive-in restaurants. In
the words of one U.S. veteran, these amen-
ities "made the rear a warm, insulated,
womblike capsule" into which the horrors
of war rarely intruded.

THE SHADOW OF THE BOMB

Two decades after the Treaty of Versailles concluded the most terrible bloodletting in human history, most people still thought of war as a horror that happened somewhere else. The memories of loss during the Great War were vivid enough—13 percent of the male population of France between the ages of fifteen and fifty were gone, with equivalent figures of 12 percent for Germany, 9 percent for Italy, and 6 percent for Britain. In all, perhaps 10 million men had died as a direct result of combat and a like number as an indirect consequence. Still, it had been a struggle of soldiers and sailors and a comparative handful of aviators. For the most part, civilians paid only with heartbreak and economic tribulation.

But that would change. Another kind of war—ancient in some respects, but carried out with weapons more dreadful than any known before—would fasten itself on the world like a nightmarish plague. Its nature was defined on April 26, 1937, in the obscure Basque town of Guernica in northeastern Spain.

For many months Spain had been racked by internal warfare, a right-versus-left struggle that pitted a rebellious army under Generalissimo Francisco Franco against the country's Republican government. But outsiders played a critical role. German chancellor Adolf Hitler and Italian dictator Benito Mussolini contributed forces to support Franco and his Nationalists; the Soviet Union—and volunteers from a number of other nations—fought on the Republican side. Spain descended into a hell of death, rape, and pillaging. Atrocities were committed without apology by both Nationalists and Republicans.

Control of the skies over the bleeding land lay mostly with the main German contingent located in Spain, a 6,000-man air force known as the Condor Legion that had been sent there by Hitler to test his new aircraft under battle conditions. In killing terms, the Condor Legion and its planes performed with unforgettable efficiency—especially at Guernica.

The war had drawn close to the Basque market town by April 26. Nationalists were approaching from the south, and Republican troops were withdrawing toward the west. In the course of their retreat, some of the Republicans were sure to use the small stone bridge that spanned the Oca River at Guernica. The bridge was, therefore, a legitimate military target.

Guernica's ordeal began at 4:30 in the afternoon, when a German bomber appeared overhead, probing local defenses. The town had none. Soon thereafter, a wave of bombers—Heinkel-111s and Junkers-52s—arrived on the scene and dropped their burden of explosives. The 550-pound bombs of one plane landed in the town plaza. Remembered one survivor, "A group of women and children were lifted high into the air, maybe twenty feet or so, and they started to break up. Legs, arms, heads, and bits and pieces started flying everywhere." The bombers swung

Homeless and abandoned, a child cries amid the ruins of a Shanghai railroad station following a surprise attack by Japanese aircraft in 1937. The use of bombers in warfare greatly increased the proportion of civilian to military casualties. To the Japanese leadership in the late 1930s, intent on gaining access to the oil and rubber resources of Southeast Asia, such distinctions in any case mattered little: Atrocities committed by their troops occupying the Chinese city of Nanjing were deliberately calculated to weaken enemy morale.

away, only to return eight more times at intervals of twenty minutes. "We bombed it and bombed it and bombed it, and *bueno,* why not?" said a Nationalist officer later. As the tons of explosives poured down, wooden buildings were blasted into splinters. Stone structures burst apart. Bombs hit a hotel, the railroad station, and then a hospital, killing the doctors, nurses, and wounded soldiers within. Incendiary devices spilled molten metal over the town, starting countless fires. When the people fled from their burning homes, Heinkel-51 fighters screamed down from above, spewing machine-gun fire on them. Soon the streets were filled with the bodies of men, women, children, and animals. By the time the attack had ended, 70 percent of Guernica had been destroyed. Of the town's population of 7,000, about 1,600 had been killed and another 900 wounded.

The world's press reported this massacre of the innocents in tones of utter outrage. But the war went on without a pause, continuing to visit devastation on civilian Spain. By the time a victorious Franco was installed as dictator two years later, almost one million Spaniards had died.

This was the future—as it was the distant past, reminiscent of the Dark Ages, when all the individuals of a society were at risk, hardly less threatened by death than those who were assigned the role of fighting. Once again, war refused to be confined: The battlefield could be anywhere, and in the years ahead, it would sometimes seem to be everywhere. Social and psychological barriers that had separated armies and civilians would dissolve, melting away in a world-engulfing fire. The nineteenth-century Prussian military theorist Carl von Clausewitz had foreseen this eventuality: War, he wrote, had been "set free from conventional trammels by the intervention of the whole people."

Ironically, the destructiveness of the First World War had prompted numerous efforts to restrain aggression and set limits on any fighting that did break out. Germany had been disarmed—denied an air force, forbidden to manufacture planes and submarines, allowed an army of only 100,000. Britain swiftly demobilized its armed forces in 1918 and dismantled its war industries. The great naval powers settled on clearly defined ratios of capital ships: The United States and Britain could have 5 to every 3 for Japan and 1.6 for France and Germany. France adopted a military doctrine that emphasized defense over offense: One result was the construction of the supposedly impregnable Maginot line, an 87-mile-long string of underground forts, tank traps, barbed wire, and other forms of static defense along the border with Germany—in effect, a supertrench.

Meanwhile, schemes of military prohibition were devised. In 1923, for example, international jurists convened at The Hague to draw up rules specifying where

U.S. B-26 Marauder bombers begin their homeward run after dropping their payloads on the rail yards and power station of the German-occupied Belgian town of Charleroi in April 1944. Toward the end of World War II, the U.S. and British air forces began around-the-clock air raids on German towns, their targets including workers' housing as well as military and industrial centers. This policy of "city busting" dented Germany's capacity to wage war and relieved the pressure on other fronts: Some 25 percent of German artillery and ammunition production was committed to air defense.

A train burns after a Boer attack in South Africa in 1901, part of a campaign to sabotage lines of communication and deprive the occupying British troops of essential supplies. The British, unused to such tactics, resorted to rounding up Boer families and burning their farms in order to defeat them.

Armed with an antiquated German rifle, a French resistance fighter hides in a tree in Normandy during the Second World War. A clandestine leaflet warned recruits hoping to join the struggle against the occupying Nazis that they would "live badly, in precarious fashion, with food hard to find."

In Vietnam, Communist guerrillas prepare a booby trap consisting of a log studded with bamboo spikes. Often smeared with excrement to ensure that any resulting wound would become infected, such improvised weapons were successfully deployed against the far-better-armed South Vietnamese and U.S. forces.

GUERRILLAS: THE PEOPLE FIGHT BACK

A guerrilla force should be "intangible, without back or front, drifting about like a gas." So wrote the Englishman T. E. Lawrence, who successfully led an irregular Arab force against the Turks in the First World War. French troops in Spain during the Peninsula War in the early nineteenth century would have recognized this description: They were constantly provoked by bands of resistance fighters who vanished into the hills after each attack. Guerrilla means "small war" in Spanish—but though small in scale, guerrilla actions have played a major part in twentieth-century warfare.

Guerrilla fighting involves the protracted harassment by a weaker force of a stronger one—usually an informal civilian corps contending with the army of a foreign invader or repressive government. Skillful guerrillas compensate for their lack of numbers and equipment with other advantages: They often know the terrain better than their enemy, have the support of the local population, and—because they have no front line to hold—can make surprise attacks on their enemy's weakest point whenever they choose. "Deliver a lightning blow," urged Mao Zedong in his classic manual, *On Guerrilla Warfare*. The fate of captured guerrillas has traditionally been execution, and they have commonly treated their own prisoners in the same way—a cycle of violence that makes for a particularly brutal form of warfare.

In El Salvador in 1982, men and women receive training in guerrilla tactics. At the height of the fighting in 1981 and 1982, both left-wing guerrillas and right-wing death squads were operating in the suburbs of the capital city, San Salvador.

bombers could strike. "Aerial bombardment," they solemnly concluded, "is legitimate only when directed at a military objective." (Unfortunately, however, the jurists could not agree on the definition of "military objective.") The foreign ministers of the principal European powers signed the Locarno Pact in 1925, guaranteeing existing borders in western Europe. And in 1928, a total of fifteen governments, including the United States, Britain, France, Germany, Italy, and Japan, were signatories of the Kellogg-Briand Pact, which condemned "recourse to war for the solution of international controversies" and renounced it "as an instrument of national policy in their relations with one another."

But the ingredients of war—trained military forces, ample armaments, and perceived reasons for using them—did not disappear. The pacific hopes of the 1920s were widely seen to be a mirage by the middle of the next decade, although denial would run strong in Europe until the very moment Hitler unleashed his rebuilt arsenal. Beyond the bounds of Europe, in any case, the flames of war blazed up repeatedly. In 1935, for instance, Mussolini, covetous of a colonial empire, attacked Ethiopia with ten divisions and a supporting force of nearly 400 planes. Because Ethiopia had an air force of just 12 planes, Italian aircraft were able to punish the opposing ground troops with shrapnel bombs and gas. Nonetheless, Italy took seven months to complete the job of conquest.

A far more potent aggressor was stirring in the Far East. In the early 1930s, Japan's government fell under the domination of military leaders. This officer caste had powerful tools to work with. The nation's regular army numbered some 300,000, and there were more than two million trained reservists; in addition, Japan's navy was the third largest in the world, and one of the best equipped. They did not hesitate to put these formidable forces to use. In 1932, Japan seized Manchuria, a coal- and iron-rich region that was nominally part of China. That ancient, immense country was suffering the pangs of a bitter civil war, waged by Mao Zedong's Communists and the landlord-dominated Nationalist party of Jiang Jieshi (Chiang Kai-shek), and was in no position to defend the region. Japan's military leaders noted the weakness, and were determined to exploit it further.

Along with their impressive armory, Japan's rulers had sweeping ambitions for their country. Japan, they believed, was East Asia's natural bulwark against the West and its alien, exploitive ways. But to realize its destiny as the only force that could counter the imperial acquisitiveness of the West, Japan needed to solve various internal difficulties. Overcrowding was one: Crammed into its mountainous islands were 80 million people, and one million were being added each year. Japan was not only the most crowded nation in the world, it was also sorely lacking in natural resources. But its huge and weak neighbor had both space and raw materials in abundance. For the sake of Asia's well-being, therefore, China must be taken.

Nor was the justification merely economic: Conquest would strengthen not only Japan but China itself by inculcating Japan's supposedly superior values and culture. Japan would cite the same arguments for later invasions. Burma and Malaya, which at that time belonged to Great Britain, were needed for their valuable resources of tin, tungsten, and bauxite; Indochina, part of France's colonial empire, possessed rich rubber plantations; the East Indies, then controlled by the Dutch, had oil. These territories and more would be folded into what Japan's leaders would call a "Greater East Asia Co-Prosperity Sphere," an immense empire to which the aggressors felt they were divinely entitled.

At first, subduing China seemed easy. In July 1937, Japanese armies swept down from the north, brushing aside resistance and seizing railroad lines and cities. By December, they had reached Nanjing, the Nationalist capital. Jiang Jieshi and his government withdrew, leaving the city to the invaders and moving deeper into China to fight another day.

But for the Japanese, simply possessing the enemy's capital was not enough. The force occupying Nanjing was ordered to deal with the population in a manner that would strike terror in Nationalists everywhere and dissuade them from further resistance. Over the next two months, the Japanese soldiers indulged in an orgy of cruelty comparable with the vengeful rampages of the Mongols seven centuries earlier. Thousands of buildings were put to the torch. Looting was unrestrained. Mass rapes, followed by mutilations and killings, occurred in the refugee camps around the city, in the hospitals, and in Chinese women's colleges.

Chinese men of military age were used for bayonet practice, mowed down with machine guns, or doused with gasoline and set on fire. When word of these deeds spread through the Japanese imperial command, some officers wept with shame. But it would happen again as the Japanese pursued their dreams of conquest, though never on such a scale: A postwar investigation of the agony of Nanjing revealed that 20,000 women had been raped and as many as 200,000 people killed.

Europe would see worse, a consequence of the virulent racism and expansionist fantasies of Adolf Hitler and his Nazis, who would form an alliance with the Japanese in 1940. Hitler came to power in 1933, winning the chancellorship by a combination of political violence and brilliant oratory that fed on economic disarray in Germany and deep resentment of the punitive Treaty of Versailles. He saw himself as a man of destiny, and a number of his beliefs echoed those voiced in Japan. In his political manifesto, *Mein Kampf,* he wrote that the Nazi party "must attempt to remove the disproportion between our population and our living space *and* between our historical past and the hopelessness of our present impotence."

Elsewhere in the same feverish document, he claimed a kind of divine sanction for doing whatever it took to secure "the existence of our race and nation, the sustenance of its children and the purity of its blood, the freedom and independence of the fatherland, and the nation's ability to fulfill the mission appointed to it by the creator of the universe." Germans were the master race, he believed; all other peoples were inferior, and some—Jews, Gypsies, Slavs—were subhuman. He proposed to reorder the world, spreading Nazi values, seizing land for German settlement, and removing or subjugating peoples as needed.

His primary territorial ambitions lay to the east, and the population there would bear the brunt of his malignity. In the months and years after he started the Second World War with the invasion of Poland on September 1, 1939, one and one-half million Poles were expelled from their country's western and southern provinces; 200,000 Polish children of possible German ancestry (or who were merely Aryan in appearance) were kidnapped and taken to Germany to enrich the bloodstock of the fatherland; 200,000 people from the Baltic provinces were deported to the Soviet Union; Jews were forced into ghettos, then concentration camps, and eventually killed by the millions. Even more sweeping acts of genocide were imagined: Heinrich Himmler, head of the *Schutzstaffel* (SS), estimated that 30 million Slavs would have to be exterminated to open up Russia for resettlement by Germanic peoples.

Pity and mercy obviously had no place in all of this, but Hitler obscured the horrors that he planned, telling his commanders at the outset, "Things will be done of which German generals would not approve." Much of the dirty work would be assigned to special SS death squads. In Poland, they executed aristocrats, priests, teachers, merchants, and government officials—anyone who, in their opinion, might lead the opposition. In Russia, the death squads set new standards for slaughter. Said one routine SS report in 1941, "About 500 Jews, among other saboteurs, are currently being liquidated every day." When a hotel was blown up in Kiev, 33,000 Jews were killed in reprisal. In a single day at Pinsk, 16,000 Jews were killed with pistols, grenades, clubs, axes, and dogs.

It had to be done, Hitler believed. By the same token, he had long assumed that the German people would have to endure a war with both East and West in order to gain their rightful future. But he had expected it to be a short struggle—and for a time, this looked likely. In the first year of the war, his fast-moving columns of armor and infantry, supported by swarms of fighters and dive bombers, sliced through the opposition with astonishing ease. Poland fell in a month, France in six weeks, Denmark in two days, Norway in two months, Belgium in seventeen days, Holland in five days, Yugoslavia in eleven days, Greece in three weeks. In skilled hands, it seemed, up-to-date weaponry—tanks, single-wing aircraft, fast-firing artillery, radios to link all the forces—offered a dramatically efficient alternative to the mode of war that had cost Europe much of its young manhood two decades earlier. If not painless, the new style of war was at least quick.

But Hitler overreached himself on June 22, 1941, when he sent his armies into the Russian vastness that had swallowed Napoleon. And in the Far East, Japan's military

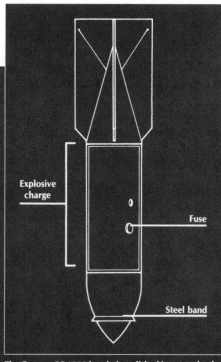

As shown here and on the following pages, the Second World War was characterized by an awesome escalation in the technology of airborne destruction. The German bombers that attacked London during the Blitz of 1940 and 1941 caused serious damage and loss of life in local areas *(far right)*, but could only temporarily disrupt the life of a large city. Britain and the United States subsequently developed much larger bombers and could muster more than 1,000 such aircraft for a single raid. By 1944, Germany had produced the V-2 rocket, a forerunner of the intercontinental ballistic missile. By 1945, a lone American plane was able to annihilate an entire Japanese city with just one bomb scarcely larger than the 4,000-pound bomb shown here.

ANNIHILATION FROM THE AIR

The German SC 1800 bomb demolished its target by the force of its explosion. The steel band around the nose was designed to prevent penetration on impact and thus obtain maximum damage aboveground.

leaders committed an error no less grave. To prevent any American interference with their territorial ambitions, they bombed the U.S. Pacific Fleet at Pearl Harbor on December 7, 1941. In so doing, they found themselves locked in a death struggle with a nation whose resources far exceeded their own. On December 11, Hitler declared war on the United States as well.

The demon of institutionalized death was now fully unleashed and would rage unchecked until 1945. Some 50 million men, women, and children would die. Their lives would be taken by tanks, cannon, rifles, machine guns, mortars, grenades, flamethrowers, mines, submarines, surface ships, aircraft, rockets, Cyclon-B gas, and a hundred other tools of destruction. Many millions would die of cold, disease, and starvation. The majority of victims were noncombatants—70 percent of the total, as compared with 45 percent in World War I.

Civilian populations were especially vulnerable to bombers, usually arrayed in fleets similar to the assemblage that dropped thousands of tons of explosives on the little Basque town of Guernica. On two occasions, however, large cities would be blasted into oblivion by single bombs that loosed the power of the atom. Those two staggering blows—the ultimate extension of strategic bombing—would alter the enterprise of war forever.

The military value of aerial bombing had first been considered in detail in a book entitled *The Command of the Air,* published by an Italian theorist named Giulio Douhet in 1921. Air power, said Douhet, would win the next war, because only airplanes could disregard lines of battle and "inflict upon the enemy attacks of a terrifying nature to which he can in no way react." Another prophet of bombing was

Members of a German aircrew cautiously connect an SC 1800 bomb to suspension brackets beneath a Heinkel-111 bomber. To prevent a premature explosion, the bomb was detonated by an electrical fuse timed to explode on impact.

Rescue teams clear the ruins of the ticket office at a subway station in the financial district of London, following a direct hit by an SC 1800 bomb dropped on the night of January 11, 1941. The bomb killed more than fifty people and closed a seven-road intersection, but within three weeks, a temporary bridge had been erected and traffic was moving again.

Hugh Montague Trenchard, chief of the British air staff after World War I. He believed, along with Douhet, that there was no effective defense against bombers and that they would have a devastating effect on civilian morale. In America, the same message was articulated by William "Billy" Mitchell of the U.S. Army Air Service, who spoke of attacks that would destroy the cities, factories, and food supplies of an enemy, shattering the will to fight.

Military men were not in agreement with such views, but politicians and the public listened. As Nazi bellicosity spread its chill in the 1930s, the presumed horrors of aerial assault bombing were portrayed in such works of fiction as *The Gas War of 1940*, *Invasion from the Air,* and *War Upon Women*. The ill-advised efforts of British governments to appease Hitler during the years that led up to World War II were motivated at least in part by a dread of Luftwaffe bombers. Most of Britain's leadership agreed with the despairing assessment offered by Prime Minister Stanley Baldwin early in the decade: "The man in the street," said Baldwin, should "realize that there is no power on earth that can protect him from being bombed. . . . The bomber will always get through." Shortly after the war began, the Imperial Defense Committee predicted that 600,000 people would die in a German bombing campaign, and more than one million would be wounded.

This forecast was tested when the Luftwaffe began bombing Britain in the summer of 1940. The first targets were radar stations and air bases. Because of the effectiveness of Britain's early-warning system and the skill of Royal Air Force (RAF) fighter pilots, the Germans lost far more aircraft than they had anticipated. Then, Britain struck a retaliatory blow that Germany's rulers never expected: Defying the Reich's air defenses, British planes managed to drop a few bombs on Berlin.

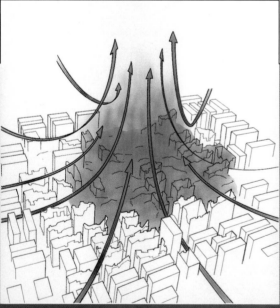

A firestorm occurs when individual fires that have been caused by widespread bombing combine into a major conflagration—the heat generated by the blaze creates a column of rapidly rising hot air, which sucks cool air into the center of the inferno, causing high winds that fan and intensify the existing flames.

A British Avro Lancaster drops a high-explosive bomb and a cluster of incendiaries. The high explosives would demolish roofs and blow in windows, allowing the incendiaries to lodge within and incinerate the buildings. If used without high explosives, the incendiaries were apt to slide off angled roofs into the street, where they could be extinguished more easily.

Up to that point, Hitler had focused on bombing military targets. Now, he promised to teach the British a lesson for their audacious act. "When they declare that they will increase their attacks on our cities, then we will raze their cities to the ground. We will stop the handiwork of these night air pirates, so help us God! When the British air force drops 3,000 or 4,000 kilograms of bombs, then we will, in one raid, drop 300,000 or 400,000 kilograms."

The Luftwaffe took the war to London. For seventy-six consecutive nights with a single intermission, bombs rained down on the city. The biggest raids claimed upward of 1,000 lives and rendered ten times that number homeless. But the aerial assault was not the catastrophe that had been feared—and ironically, it had the effect of stiffening British resolve.

Meanwhile, RAF raids against Germany were going poorly. So few bombs hit their targets that when Winston Churchill was presented with an RAF proposal for a vast enlargement of its bomber fleet, he responded, "It is very disputable whether bombing by itself will be a factor in the present war. On the contrary, all that we have

In Europe, the Allies launched a day-and-night bombing campaign designed to undermine the enemy's ability to wage war by destroying industry, disrupting transportation, and weakening civilian morale. A calculated combination of explosive and incendiary bombs produced firestorms that raged through both industrial and residential districts. Japanese cities, having a preponderance of highly flammable wooden buildings, suffered even more from this phenomenon than did German cities. The scale of destruction worried even its perpetrators: the British prime minister Winston Churchill warned that "we shall come into control of an utterly ruined land."

A stone figure atop Dresden town hall looks down on the eerie stillness of the ruined city after raids by 772 British and 311 American bombers on February 13 and 14, 1945. The city burned for one week, after the initial firestorm engulfed an area of 1,600 acres and sucked the air from shelters. The death toll numbered 35,000.

learned since the war began shows that its effects, both physical and moral, are greatly exaggerated. The most we can say is that it will be a heavy and I trust seriously increasing annoyance."

That the majority of the victims would be members of the noncombatant population of cities was now obvious. Churchill explicitly stated that bombing should destroy not only "war production in all of its forms"—factories, oil fields, transportation centers—but also the "life and economy of the whole of that guilty organization." The United States had initially expressed abhorrence of such an inclusive policy. Back in September 1939, President Franklin D. Roosevelt had addressed an "urgent appeal to every government that may be engaged in hostilities publicly to affirm its determination that its armed forces shall in no event, and under no circumstances, undertake the bombardment from the air of civilian populations or of unfortified cities." But when America entered the war, political and military leaders began to see things otherwise. Saturation bombing—the targeting of large areas rather than individual factories or the like—came to be regarded as a necessary evil that would shorten the war.

The scale of the air war was staggering. At its peak strength, the U.S. Army Air Forces had 2.4 million personnel and nearly 80,000 planes. Britain's RAF had nearly 1.2 million members by the end of the war. Given such resources, a single raid could utterly overwhelm the air defenses of a city. On the night of May 30, 1942, for example, RAF Bomber Command sent forth more than 1,000 bombers to strike Cologne, Germany's third-largest city and an important manufacturing center on the Rhine River. Heading across the North Sea, the bombers formed a great stream sixty-eight miles in length. Mechanical difficulties caused some planes to turn back,

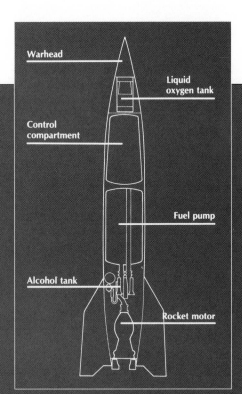

The liquid oxygen and alcohol fuel of the V-2 rocket burned for just seventy seconds, sending the missile with its 2,000-pound warhead into the atmosphere at a speed of more than 4,000 miles per hour.

Warhead

Liquid oxygen tank

Control compartment

Fuel pump

Alcohol tank

Rocket motor

A V-2 rocket is raised on its launch apparatus in September 1945. The secrets of rocket technology were eagerly sought by both the Americans and the Soviets after the war ended, and German scientists who had worked on the V-2 were to play a leading role in subsequent ballistic missile and space rocket development.

and German fighters further reduced their numbers, but when the fleet reached Cologne, it still possessed crushing strength.

For more than one hour, wave after wave of bombers dropped their burden of explosives—1,600 tons in all. The citizens of Cologne—who had already endured 106 earlier bombing raids—watched aghast as their city was pulverized and an area three miles long by almost two miles wide was set ablaze. Planes arriving in the later waves had to release their 1,000- and 4,000-pound bombs into a column of smoke rising more than 16,000 feet high. By the time the last bomber had turned for home, 250 factories had been destroyed or damaged, 45,000 people were homeless, and 474 people were dead.

For all the fury of the attack, the death toll at Cologne paled in comparison with civilian deaths in the firestorms that bombers ignited in several cities during the war. The first occurred in Hamburg on the night of July 27, 1943. Previous raids had burst water mains and impaired the firefighting capacity of the city. As a result, fires started by incendiary bombs raged out of control and merged. The heat caused great masses of air to rise. Cool air rushed in to replace it, creating winds of up to 155 miles an hour and turning the city into an inferno. Cars were flung about; asphalt streets burst into flame as temperatures reached about 1,800° F.; people huddling in shelters suffocated from the lack of oxygen or were burned alive. In the nine-day assault on Hamburg of which the raid was a part, almost ten square miles of the city was destroyed. An estimated 50,000 people died.

In February 1945, a similar fate befell Dresden, a historic and lovely city of little military importance, but possessing rail yards and oil installations. The RAF Bomber Command struck on a clear night, sending 772 planes in two waves and dropping

An area of flattened houses in the London suburb of Highgate in November 1944 bears witness to the destructive power of the V-2 rocket. During the period between September 1944 and the end of the war, 1,190 V-2 rockets were launched against the British capital, killing more than 2,700 people.

As the war drew to a close, the Germans introduced a series of *Vergeltungswaffen*—"retaliation weapons"—that included the V-1 flying bomb and the V-2 rocket. Propelled through the air by the force of its rocket engine, the V-2 was launched on a preset trajectory and had a range of about 200 miles. Because the rocket traveled faster than sound, its approach would be heard only after its detonation—thus giving no warning of its arrival. A British prime minister's prewar fear that the "bomber would always get through" was most truly fulfilled by this weapon: There was no defense against it other than the capture or destruction of its launch sites.

almost 3,000 tons of bombs, three-quarters of them incendiary. There was no opposition—Germany by then was almost finished. In the wake of the attack, thousands of separate fires lighted by the bombs joined in a single hurricane of fire, incinerating 2.5 square miles of old Dresden and spreading death into the nooks and crannies where people sought refuge.

A schoolteacher who later came to help deal with the disaster described the horror that he encountered: "Never had I expected to see people interred in that state: burned, cremated, torn, and crushed to death; sometimes the victims looked like ordinary people apparently peacefully sleeping; the faces of others were racked with pain, the bodies stripped almost naked by the tornado; there were wretched refugees from the East clad only in rags, and people from the Opera in all their finery; here the victim was a shapeless slab, there a layer of ashes shoveled into a zinc tub." An estimated 35,000 people died.

Germany was not alone in glimpsing the apocalypse. After midnight on March 10, 1945, as the forces of the United States closed in on Japan, a group of B-29 bombers dropped incendiaries on Tokyo, a 193-square-mile tinderbox of wood and paper houses. Multitudinous fires were whipped into a single stupendous conflagration that devoured more than 15 square miles of the city, caused water in the canals to boil, and generated such air turbulence that bombers at 6,500 feet were flipped over. More than 100,000 inhabitants of the city died, one million were injured, and another one million lost their homes.

Despite its extreme violence, saturation bombing did not break the fighting spirit of target nations or so damage their economies as to make further fighting impossible.

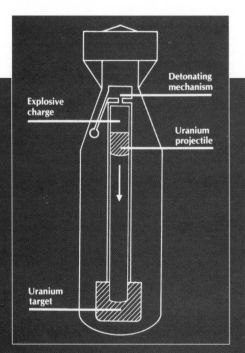

The atomic bomb Little Boy was detonated by the firing of a small piece of uranium into a larger piece at a speed of 2,750 feet per second. The resultant chain reaction of colliding and splitting atoms caused an explosion equivalent to that of 20,000 tons of TNT.

Measuring just under ten feet, Little Boy awaits loading at a U.S. air base located on an island in the Pacific Ocean. To prevent a premature explosion, the bomb had a three-switch detonation sequence: The first switch was triggered when the bomb was released from the plane; the second was activated by air pressure at 4,900 feet; the third was operated by a radar device that initiated an electrical impulse at about 1,900 feet—the height at which, it was calculated, the bomb would cause maximum damage to the city below.

By the last year of the war, urban Germany was mostly rubble, but the damage did more to stoke hatred of the Allies than to cow or demoralize the victims. City dwellers displayed extraordinary resilience. Less than a month after the 1,000-plane raid on Cologne in 1942, the city was back to near-normal. One year after four-fifths of Hamburg had been destroyed by firestorm in 1943, two-thirds of the population had returned. War production showed a similar ability to survive the aerial pounding, in large part because Germany had a conscript force of six million laborers—prisoners of war and recruits from occupied lands—who were used to repair damaged facilities, move whole factories to safer areas, or even build factories underground. German war production actually increased between 1942 and 1944, although late in the war, the bombing of oil installations caused serious difficulties.

Nor did the saturation bombing bring about victory in the Pacific theater, although fleets of American bombers bludgeoned Japan relentlessly during the last two years of the conflict. The great Ōsaka harbor complex was hammered into a smoldering ruin. The city of Nagoya was devastated. By the spring of 1945, hundreds of bombers were appearing over Japan two days out of every three. Seven different targets were attacked by 400 bombers on May 10. The imperial palace was burned during a raid on Tokyo on May 24. Half of the city of Yokohama was leveled on May 29. By July, Japan had been hit by almost 100,000 tons of bombs. The air raids had set fire to a total of 127 square miles across twenty-six cities. War material production had dropped to 40 percent of its 1944 peak. The bombing had killed 500,000 people and destroyed the homes of 13 million. Among the civilians, however, the will to fight was hardly dimmed. A journalist wrote: "In the heart of the ordinary Japanese, there was hatred and bitterness toward the American raiders who left an indiscriminate trail

Stunned survivors wander in the wasteland that was once the city of Hiroshima, destroyed in the world's first atomic-bomb attack. The heat at ground zero, the point on the ground directly below the explosion, reached 10,800° F.: The surface of granite building stones up to 3,000 feet away melted. Said one eyewitness: "It seemed impossible that such a scene could have been caused by human means."

The bomb you are going to drop," the crew of the U.S. B-29 bomber *Enola Gay* was told on August 4, 1945, "is something new in the history of warfare. It is the most destructive ever produced." Two days later, the world's first operational atomic bomb, known as Little Boy, was dropped on the Japanese city of Hiroshima. The heat and blast it generated—thousands of times more powerful than those of a conventional bomb—killed nearly 80,000 civilians immediately. A like number died of radiation-related illnesses during the following five years. The use of the bomb caused deep uneasiness among some American officers, one of whom noted that it seemed to signal a return to the barbarity of the Dark Ages.

of blackened corpses of babies and grandmothers among the wreckage of war."

As for the military leaders of Japan, they subscribed to a code called Bushido, or "the way of the warrior." This ethical system exalted iron discipline and self-control, the endurance of any hardship, the carrying out of any order, no matter how impossible. Honor was supremely important. To be taken prisoner was an utter disgrace. To surrender was punishable by death. As a consequence, their course was clear—they would fight to the end.

But the United States had a terrible card to play, and bombing would finally achieve what the prophets of aerial warfare had foreseen. Ever since the early years of the century, scientists had known that powerful forces lurked in the invisible world of atoms—building blocks of matter so small that many billions exist in a grain of sand. In 1938, two German scientists managed to split the nucleus of nature's biggest

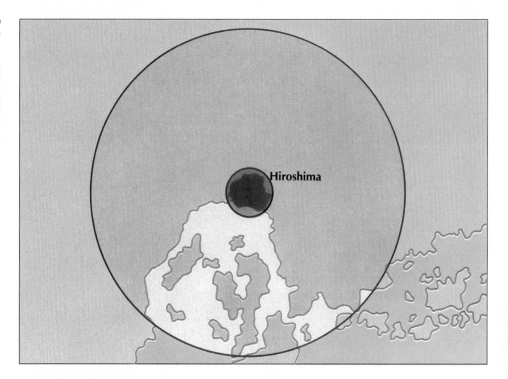

The inner ring superimposed on this map of a portion of the southern coast of Japan shows the extent of damage—buildings either demolished or partially destroyed—inflicted on Hiroshima by the atomic bomb dropped in 1945. That bomb had an explosive force of approximately twenty kilotons; most modern nuclear weapons have warheads of one to five megatons, but some are vastly more powerful. (A kiloton is equivalent to 1,000 tons of TNT, a megaton to one million tons.) The outer circle, with a radius of about twenty miles, indicates the probable area of destruction that would result from the dropping of a twenty-megaton bomb.

atom, that of uranium. In the process, energy was released—vastly more energy than could be generated by chemical reactions. (Subsequent calculations indicated that nuclear fission, as the process of splitting an atomic nucleus became known, would produce 40 million times as much energy as the maximum achievable by chemical means, including the combustion of conventional bombs.)

Word of what the Germans had done spread quickly, and before long, physicists in Britain, France, the United States, and Japan were engaged in similar experiments. At Columbia University in New York City in 1939, Leo Szilard, a Hungarian refugee from the Nazis, demonstrated that fission released neutrons, subatomic particles that could split the nuclei of other atoms, releasing still more neutrons—and so on, in a self-sustaining chain reaction. "That night," said Szilard, "I knew the world was headed for sorrow."

Soon, however, physicists discovered that self-sustaining fission was possible only with U-235, an isotope that constituted a tiny fraction of naturally occurring uranium, or with a new element called plutonium, which could be created by bombarding the principal uranium isotope, U-238, with neutrons. To acquire meaningful amounts of either substance posed prodigiously difficult problems of physics, chemistry, and engineering. During the war years, only the United States had the resources and scientific wherewithal (let alone the brainpower of dozens of physicists who had fled the Nazis) to pull it off. The American effort, known as the Manhattan Project, cost more than $2 billion and at its height enlisted the services of 600,000 people, all working under conditions designed to keep the secret of a fission weapon safe.

At 5:30 a.m. on July 16, 1945, an atomic bomb made of plutonium was successfully tested at the Alamogordo bombing range in New Mexico. Hundreds of miles

Details of U.S. nuclear-missile and bomber bases are projected onto screens during a training exercise in the command post of the U.S. Eighth Air Force, located in Los Angeles. Linked by integrated computers to the North American Air Defense Command headquarters deep within the Colorado mountains, control rooms such as this coordinate some 10,000 strategic nuclear weapons and the missile silos, bombers, and submarines designed to launch them. They also constantly monitor the Soviet Union by satellite and radar station for warning of any possible missile attack.

away, people thought that an earthquake had occurred or that a giant meteorite had struck nearby. The light of the explosion would have been visible on Mars. At that same time, the American president Harry Truman was at Potsdam—on the outskirts of Berlin—discussing postwar policies with Winston Churchill and Joseph Stalin. When his aide confidentially informed him of the nuclear explosion in New Mexico, he spoke of the bomb as the "greatest thing in history." He intended to use it to end the war with Japan.

The only other way to subdue Japan—already much debated in the high councils of the U.S. government—was by an invasion of the home islands that might have cost as many as one million American casualties. U.S. Army Chief of Staff George C. Marshall subsequently spelled out the reasoning behind Truman's decision in favor of a nuclear strike, pointing out that the United States had just gone through eighty-

Two London housewives begin to assemble their newly delivered Anderson shelter in 1939. Though adequate for short daytime raids, these structures provided little comfort during prolonged nighttime bombing, because they were cold, damp, and prone to flooding.

A Londoner surveys the crater left by a bomb that has narrowly missed his Anderson shelter, buried up to its roof in his garden to give extra protection against flying debris.

TAKING COVER IN THE BLITZ

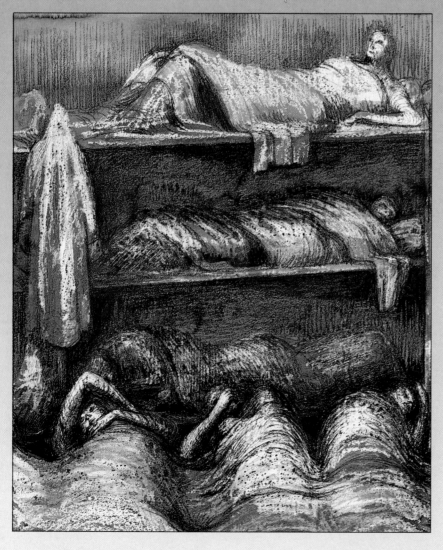

The long-suffering and at times defiant stoicism with which Londoners endured the German air offensive against their city during 1940 and 1941 typified the reaction of most urban populations that came under attack and belied the prewar theory that intensive bombing could destroy a nation's fighting spirit. Having failed to provide large public bomb shelters, the British government hastily introduced a simple corrugated-iron structure that could be erected in urban gardens—some 2.3 million of these Anderson shelters (named after the home secretary) were produced by April 1941, each providing protection for four to six people. Those caught away from their homes during an air raid took cover where they could, many of them on the station platforms of London's Underground. When sirens sounded the all clear, the weary citizens emerged into the daylight to continue their normal lives as best they could, their resolve to win the war stiffened rather than undermined.

A drawing by the British artist Henry Moore captures the cramped, claustrophobic atmosphere of the London Underground during the Blitz. Moore wrote on-the-spot notes but refrained from making sketches in the shelters—"It would have been like drawing in the hold of a slave ship," he said.

two days of savage fighting on Okinawa, a steppingstone to Japan—that campaign alone had cost the Americans 12,500 killed and missing, and the Japanese had lost 100,000. "It was expected that resistance in Japan, with their home ties, would be even more severe," said Marshall, adding that "we had the 100,000 people killed in Tokyo in one night of bombs, and it had had seemingly no effect whatsoever. . . . So it seemed quite necessary, if we could, to shock them into action. . . . We had to end the war; we had to save American lives."

On July 26, an ultimatum was broadcast from Potsdam, directed at the Japanese people and their leaders in Tokyo. It did not mention the atomic bomb, but the tone was ominous. "We call upon the government of Japan to proclaim now the unconditional surrender of all Japanese armed forces. . . . The alternative for Japan is prompt and utter destruction." Tokyo did not respond.

Early on the morning of August 6, a B-29 dubbed *Enola Gay* took off from the island of Tinian along with two escort planes and flew almost 1,500 miles to Hiroshima, a city with a population of 280,000 and a number of war material factories. The plane

approached at an altitude of 31,000 feet, released its lone weapon, and immediately veered away from the city in a violent turn. Forty-three seconds later, at 8:16:02 a.m. Hiroshima time, the bomb exploded 1,900 feet above the courtyard of a hospital. The energy released was equivalent to 20,000 tons of TNT. The *Enola Gay*, which had flown more than ten miles from the scene by then, was tossed about like a cork when the shock waves hit.

What happened directly below the explosion was erasure. An American pathologist working with an investigative team after the war offered this account: "Accompanying the flash of light was an instantaneous flash of heat. . . . Its duration was probably less than one-tenth of a second, and its intensity was sufficient to cause nearby flammable objects . . . to burst into flame and to char poles as far away as 4,000 yards from the hypocenter. At 600 to 700 yards, it was sufficient to chip and roughen granite. The heat also produced bubbling of tile to about 1,300 yards." Human beings within up to one-half mile of the fireball were transformed into unrecognizable charred, smoking bundles in less than one second. As far as 2.5 miles away, they were horribly burned. Birds burst into flame in midair.

A woman, who was five years old at the time, remembered: "People came fleeing from the nearby streets. The skin was burned off some of them and was hanging from their hands and their chins; their faces were red and so swollen that you could hardly tell where their eyes and mouths were." A train located about one mile from ground zero was twisted into a glassless tangle, all its passengers dead. People flung themselves into any water they could find and died there, either from their burns or from drowning brought about because of their weakness. Children ran through the streets, screaming for their mothers. Bodies were pinned in the wreckage of buildings, or lay torn and riddled by the glass from shattered windows.

Later a strange rain fell, huge black drops containing the radioactivity of the mushroom cloud. Within two weeks, doctors found themselves dealing with symptoms they did not understand—bloody urine, subcutaneous spots, bleeding gums, falling hair, low white-blood-cell counts. People who seemed to be recovering from their injuries in the blast began dying in large numbers. The doctors could do nothing—one of them wrote afterward, "I considered a family lucky if it had not lost more than two of its members." The dying would go on for years, steadily raising the toll of the bomb to 140,000 lives or more. As for Hiroshima the city, 62,000 of its 90,000 buildings had been destroyed.

And still Japan's military leaders appeared unwilling to surrender. So the United States repeated its message of death: Three days after the obliteration of Hiroshima, an atomic bomb was dropped on the city of Nagasaki. Although this bomb was almost twice as powerful as the first, its energy was contained by steep hills surrounding the city, and the physical damage was less devastating. But 70,000 people

Protesters call for an end to nuclear-weapons testing at a demonstration held in Trafalgar Square, London, in 1958. Among the placards displayed are those of the newly formed Campaign for Nuclear Disarmament, whose distinctive logo shows the semaphore sign *P* for peace. Public concern about the proliferation of nuclear weapons was most vehemently expressed in Western nations in the early 1960s, following the Cuban missile crisis, and during the early 1980s, when the stationing of U.S. cruise and Pershing II missiles on European soil brought more than five million demonstrators onto the streets of Europe's capital cities.

157

died in the blast and shortly afterward, and radiation poisoning would ultimately raise that toll to 140,000.

Finally, a few days later, with the Japanese government in dissolution and racked by assassinations and suicides, Emperor Hirohito stepped in. Venerated as a descendant of gods, seen as the very embodiment of the Japanese state, he normally stood above political affairs. But now, after listening to the army chief of staff say, "We have been preserving our strength, and we expect to counterattack," he spoke out. "I cannot bear to see my innocent people suffer any longer. . . . The time has come when we must bear the unbearable. I swallow my tears and give my sanction to the proposal to accept the Allied proclamation." On September 2, 1945, the Japanese surrender was formally accepted, six years and one day after Hitler had ordered his troops across the border into Poland. The war was over.

But war, of course, was not over. The international struggle that lasted from 1939 to 1945 had swept tens of millions of noncombatants into a whirlpool of destruction, and what happened at Hiroshima and Nagasaki carried war into regions of calamity almost too awful to contemplate. On a lesser scale, however, people would continue to fight often during the next five decades. Even as they did so, the nuclear specter would loom ever larger, so dreadful in its consequences that all-out war had perhaps finally become unthinkable.

National leaders would occasionally use the nuclear option for purposes of psychological warfare. When the Soviet Union sealed off occupied Berlin in 1948 in an effort to gain hegemony over the city, Truman sent two squadrons of B-29s to Germany. It was not coincidental that planes of this type had dropped the bombs on Hiroshima and Nagasaki. To reinforce the message, official news releases described the aircraft as "atomic capable," although they were not in fact equipped to carry atomic bombs—as the Soviets may have known.

While at Potsdam, Truman had jotted in his diary, "It's a good thing that Hitler's crowd or Stalin's did not discover this atomic bomb." His advisers did not expect the Soviets to develop atomic weapons for years, if ever. But on September 3, 1949, a converted B-29 bomber carrying out routine weather reconnaissance between Japan and Alaska brought back unwelcome proof that the Americans were badly mistaken. While flying over the Kamchatka Pensinula in the Northern Pacific, it picked up air samples bearing traces of exotic dust that indicated a high level of radioactivity. The evidence was unmistakable. Just over four years after the Americans had exploded their own first device, the Soviets had the bomb, too. Not only that: The samples suggested that this recently exploded bomb was a more advanced type than the one dropped by the Americans on Hiroshima. A nuclear arms race was under way.

By that time, the United States had about 200 atomic weapons, but there were reasons to think that the Soviet Union could catch up. Seeking to maintain an edge, the leaders of the United States ordered the crash development of a second-generation nuclear weapon whose workings had been outlined back in the days of the Manhattan Project. It would use a fission explosion to heat hydrogen isotopes to astronomical temperatures, causing them to fuse into helium atoms and disgorge energy in the process. The estimated explosive force of such a thermonuclear bomb would be equivalent to 10 million tons of TNT, 500 times more powerful than the bomb that devastated Hiroshima.

On November 1, 1952, the first such device was tested at Eniwetok, on the small

A CH-47 Chinook helicopter hovers above an American soldier in Vietnam. Versatile and highly maneuverable in jungle terrain, helicopters were used by U.S. forces in Vietnam as gunships, for reconnaissance, and for the transportation of troops and supplies: The twin-engined Chinook could carry up to forty-five soldiers or 27,500 pounds of equipment. The speedy evacuation of casualties by helicopter ensured that only one percent of wounded American soldiers died after reaching the hospital. But the helicopter's bulk and slow speed made it an easy target for ground attack: More than 5,600 were shot down during the course of the war in Vietnam.

THE HIDDEN CASUALTIES OF WAR

Every act of war leaves not only the dead to be mourned and the wounded to be nursed but also the homeless to be sheltered. The last comprise both those whose houses have already been destroyed and those desperate to escape the consequences of continuing aggression: In the weeks following the Iraqi invasion of Kuwait in August 1990, for example, 180,000 foreign workers, mainly Arab, fled from Iraq. Between 1980 and 1990, the number of refugees displaced by war rose threefold from an estimated 4.6 million to 15 million.

The great majority of refugees are from Third World nations and find temporary settlement in neighboring countries in Africa, the Middle East, Southeast Asia, and Central America. Pakistan, for instance, absorbed some 3 million refugees from Soviet-occupied Afghanistan during the 1980s. Often living in makeshift and unsanitary camps, refugees are a burden on economies already severely strained and can contribute to the outbreak of further conflict. The office of the UN High Commissioner for Refugees offers emergency relief when it can, providing food, water, shelter, and clothing—but the permanent resettlement of refugees can take years or even generations to effect.

Trucks loaded with personal possessions maneuver through the shattered buildings and rubble-strewn streets of the besieged Palestinian refugee camp of Chatila in Beirut in 1987, following a cease-fire agreement with Lebanese forces hostile to the refugees' presence. Many Palestinians have endured a destitute and insecure existence since the establishment of the state of Israel in 1948.

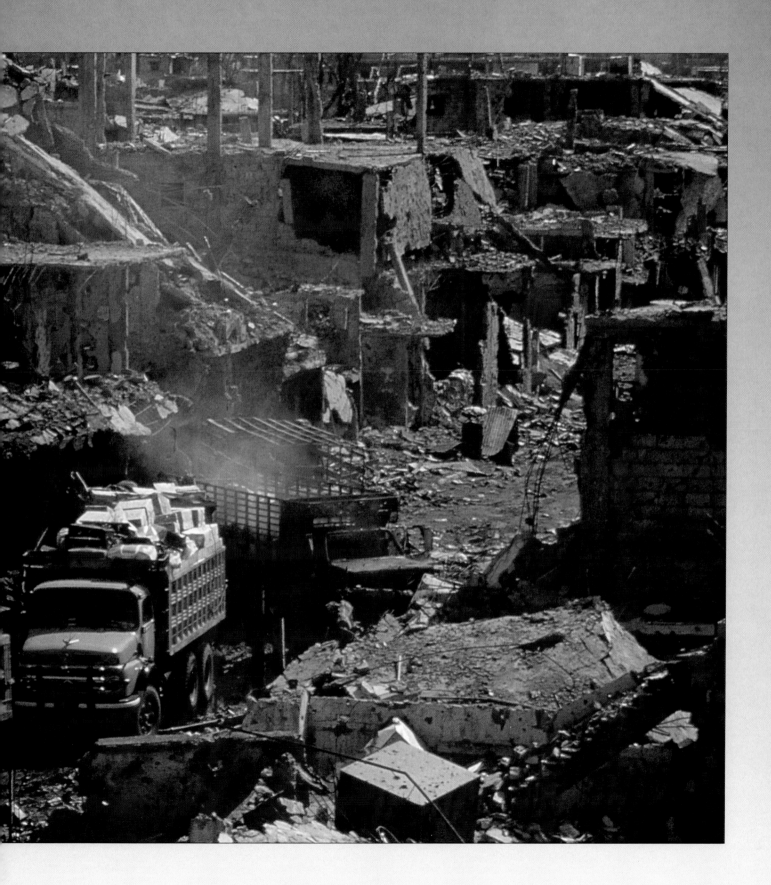

island of Elugelab in the Pacific. At the flip of a switch, a fireball three miles in diameter bloomed over the ocean. Millions of gallons of water in the island's lagoon boiled away. Elugelab was vaporized. A crater almost two miles wide and one-half mile deep had been gouged from its reef.

Once again, the United States had a weapon of unmatched power. Unfortunately for American hopes of clear nuclear superiority, the Soviet Union would conduct a thermonuclear test less than one year later.

Meanwhile, the United States rattled its nuclear saber in an effort to end the Korean War, a stalemated struggle in which America backed South Korea, and China supported the Communists of North Korea. President Truman never considered using nuclear weapons in Korea. Although he was—and remains—the only man ever to have authorized a nuclear attack, the destruction wrought on Hiroshima and Nagasaki had convinced him that the atomic bomb was no normal weapon, and he had always had doubts about its practical utility. His successor, Dwight D. Eisenhower, former supreme commander of Allied forces in Europe during World War II, had a very different view. The new president had made election promises to reduce military spending, and compared with the cost of equipping and maintaining conventional forces, atomic bombs were cheap. The warning he gave to the United Nations underlined the change from his predecessor's attitude: "Atomic weapons," he declared, "have virtually achieved conventional status within our armed forces." President Eisenhower and Secretary of State John Foster Dulles felt that intimations of a readiness to use nuclear weapons would persuade China to accept a truce, and they signaled their stance by moving warheads and suitable aircraft to Okinawa, within striking distance of both China and Korea.

Eisenhower also accepted the recommendation of his military advisers that, if armistice negotiations broke down, operations could be expanded to include "extensive strategical and tactical use of atomic bombs"—although he stressed that any such decision would be approached with great care. As things turned out, the decision was unnecessary. An armistice was signed in July 1953.

Under President Eisenhower, the possible use of nuclear weapons became an element of the basic national security policy. This included the strategy for the defense of Europe: Any large-scale conventional attack by the Soviet Union on Europe would trigger a strategic nuclear response—although, said Eisenhower, "surely no sane member of the human race could discover victory in such desolation." John Foster Dulles's phrase for the nuclear threat was "massive retaliatory power." Henceforth, he declared in 1954, the United States would deter aggression by depending "primarily upon a great capacity to retaliate, instantly, by means and at places of our own choosing."

To augment their fleets of bombers, both the United States and the Soviet Union began developing missiles. These updated versions of Hitler's V-2s could travel at many thousands of miles per hour and deliver warheads from one continent to another in thirty minutes. When they were fired from submarines close to the shores of target nations, the missiles would strike just a few minutes after launch. With the advent of these capabilities, Dulles's description of retaliation as "instant" was only a slight exaggeration.

As the potency of nuclear arms grew, the two superpowers kept approximate pace with each other. On both sides, analysts began to see that there were benefits in nuclear equality—a "delicate balance of terror," as one of them put it. If both sides possessed the ability to survive a first strike and reply with a barrage of warheads, nuclear aggression would be tantamount to suicide. U.S. Secretary of Defense Robert McNamara described the situation as "mutually assured destruction"—subsequently given the acronym MAD.

The most serious test of the delicacy of the balance occurred in October 1962, when the United States discovered from aerial reconnaissance photographs that the Soviet Union was installing nuclear missiles on the island of Cuba, just about 100 miles from American shores. President John F. Kennedy's careful response was to impose a naval blockade. The U.S. Navy would stop all vessels approaching the island and search them for nuclear missiles. (The president made sure that, for the moment, the only vessel actually searched was a Cuban ship he was reasonably certain carried no missiles.) Kennedy also warned Soviet President Nikita Khrushchev that the launching of any nuclear missile from Cuba against any part of the hemisphere would be regarded as an "attack by the Soviet Union on the United States, requiring a full retaliatory response." As a precaution, he dispersed military aircraft to civilian airfields. But there was no need—Khrushchev backed down in return for assurances that the blockade would be called off and the United States would not invade Cuba. The missiles were withdrawn.

By this time, other nations had joined the nuclear club. Britain conducted its first nuclear test in Australia in 1952. France followed suit in 1960. China and Israel developed nuclear weaponry next. By 1990, Argentina, Brazil, India, Pakistan, and South Africa were all close to possessing workable bombs.

It was estimated that the United States and the Soviet Union between them had more than 50,000 nuclear warheads. Britain, France, and China together had 1,000 to 2,000. The destructive potential of these accumulated weapons was all but incalculable—certainly exceeding one million Hiroshimas. A full-scale nuclear war might kill half the world's population, destroy the ozone layer, and thoroughly poison the planet. Humankind might cease to have a future.

In recent years, humans had nonetheless given ample evidence of their age-old inclination to solve disputes by military means. The deadly battles of Arabs and Israelis, the territorial struggles in the Falklands and the Middle East, the fierce guerrilla wars in Vietnam, Afghanistan, and Central America—these were the latest versions of human combat. The instruments of war now included jets that flew at three times the speed of sound, bombs that steered unerringly toward their targets, satellites that could see every detail on the earth hundreds of miles below, submarines able to spend months under water, ship-killing missiles, and computers to orchestrate the whole lethal array. But the fundamental nature of modern warfare would still have been familiar to peoples of other times.

In a sense, this was a reversal of the situation five decades earlier. During much of the Second World War, the limits of acceptable destruction had seemed to lose definition. At Hiroshima and Nagasaki, boundaries were found again. In 1946, the physicist Robert Oppenheimer, director of the Manhattan Project, spoke of his belief that the atomic bomb would lead to peace. "It did not take atomic weapons to make war terrible. . . . But the atomic bomb was the turn of the screw. It has made the prospect of future war unendurable. It has led us up those last few steps to the mountain pass; and beyond, there is a different country." He was at least partly right. Peace did not come, but war had to be restrained for the sake of human survival. The view from the nuclear heights changed everything.

A CONTINUING CYCLE OF CONFLICT

Between the years 1945 and 1990, while the fear of nuclear retaliation dissuaded the United States and the Soviet Union—and their respective European allies—from directly warring against each other, the rest of the world enjoyed no respite from conflict. The chart at right lists some of the more than eighty wars—fought for the most part in Asia, Africa, the Middle East, and Latin America—that claimed the lives of approximately 20 million people during that period of time.

A high proportion of the wars fought prior to 1975 were liberation struggles waged against European colonial powers: The bloodiest took place in Indochina and Algeria. Almost all of these hostilities resulted in victory for the former colonies—but many of the newly independent nations then divided along sectarian lines and descended into the turmoil of civil conflict.

The collapse of European empires—whose creation of artificial nations by drawing straight lines on maps was a major cause of subsequent conflicts—overlapped the rise of American and Soviet ambitions. Wary of direct confrontation, each of the superpowers sought to intimidate the other by building up a network of client states, either by sending military aid or by intervening in local wars. Usually, the result of this involvement was a rise in the death toll for no appreciable gain: The United States eventually withdrew from Vietnam and the Soviet Union from Afghanistan without resolving any of the issues that had precipitated the original conflicts.

Imperial or ideological fervor was in fact a less common cause of war in the nuclear age than ethnic hostility: between Arabs and Jews, Hindus and Sikhs, Iraqis and Kurds, Tamils and Sinhalese in Sri Lanka, Tutsi and Hutu in Burundi. Such enmity had deep historical roots—and while modern military hardware made for ever-longer casualty lists, modern diplomacy appeared no better able to resolve the recurrent conflicts than it had been in the past. At the beginning of the 1990s, there were fears that the dismantling of the Soviet Union—whose reach had outstripped its economic capacity—might lead to the resurfacing of similar ethnic conflicts among the previously subject peoples.

1945
Greece: civil war, to 1949.

Indonesia: war of independence, to 1948.

1946
China: civil war, to 1949.

Indochina War (Vietminh versus France), to 1954.

1947
Madagascar: colonial uprising, to 1948.

1948
Partition violence in India and Pakistan.

Arab-Israeli war, to 1949.

Malayan Emergency: guerrilla campaign against British rule, to 1960.

Burma: ethnic insurrections, continuing.

1950
Korean War (North Korea and China versus South Korea, United States, and allies), to 1953.

Indonesia: civil war, to 1965.

Chinese invasion of Tibet, to 1959.

1952
Kenya: Mau Mau rebellion, to 1956.

1954
Algeria: revolt against French rule, to 1962.

Cuba: revolution, to 1959.

1955
Cyprus: Nationalists versus Britain, and intercommunal strife between Greeks and Turks, to 1960.

1956
Soviet invasion of Hungary.

Suez crisis: Israeli, British, and French forces invade Egypt.

1959
Vietnam: North Vietnam and South Vietnam Communists versus Republic of South Vietnam and (from 1962) United States, to 1975.

1960
Congo (Zaire): civil wars, to 1965.

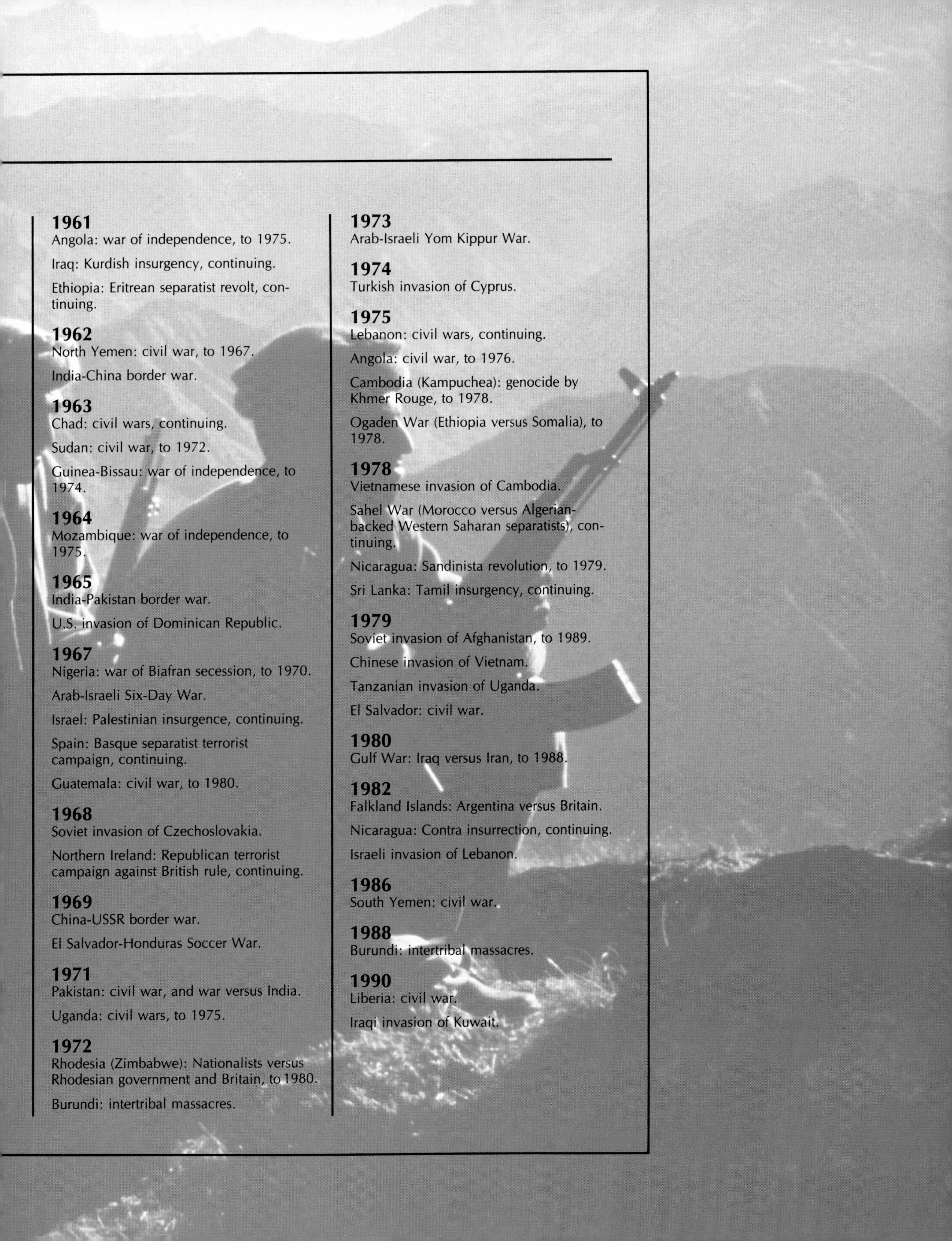

1961

Angola: war of independence, to 1975.

Iraq: Kurdish insurgency, continuing.

Ethiopia: Eritrean separatist revolt, continuing.

1962

North Yemen: civil war, to 1967.

India-China border war.

1963

Chad: civil wars, continuing.

Sudan: civil war, to 1972.

Guinea-Bissau: war of independence, to 1974.

1964

Mozambique: war of independence, to 1975.

1965

India-Pakistan border war.

U.S. invasion of Dominican Republic.

1967

Nigeria: war of Biafran secession, to 1970.

Arab-Israeli Six-Day War.

Israel: Palestinian insurgence, continuing.

Spain: Basque separatist terrorist campaign, continuing.

Guatemala: civil war, to 1980.

1968

Soviet invasion of Czechoslovakia.

Northern Ireland: Republican terrorist campaign against British rule, continuing.

1969

China-USSR border war.

El Salvador-Honduras Soccer War.

1971

Pakistan: civil war, and war versus India.

Uganda: civil wars, to 1975.

1972

Rhodesia (Zimbabwe): Nationalists versus Rhodesian government and Britain, to 1980.

Burundi: intertribal massacres.

1973

Arab-Israeli Yom Kippur War.

1974

Turkish invasion of Cyprus.

1975

Lebanon: civil wars, continuing.

Angola: civil war, to 1976.

Cambodia (Kampuchea): genocide by Khmer Rouge, to 1978.

Ogaden War (Ethiopia versus Somalia), to 1978.

1978

Vietnamese invasion of Cambodia.

Sahel War (Morocco versus Algerian-backed Western Saharan separatists), continuing.

Nicaragua: Sandinista revolution, to 1979.

Sri Lanka: Tamil insurgency, continuing.

1979

Soviet invasion of Afghanistan, to 1989.

Chinese invasion of Vietnam.

Tanzanian invasion of Uganda.

El Salvador: civil war.

1980

Gulf War: Iraq versus Iran, to 1988.

1982

Falkland Islands: Argentina versus Britain.

Nicaragua: Contra insurrection, continuing.

Israeli invasion of Lebanon.

1986

South Yemen: civil war.

1988

Burundi: intertribal massacres.

1990

Liberia: civil war.

Iraqi invasion of Kuwait.

EUROPE

10,000 BC–AD 500

Greek infantry, drawn up in the battle formation known as the phalanx, defeat the much larger army of the Persian king Darius I at Marathon (490 BC).

Alexander the Great begins a thirteen-year campaign of conquest that will establish his reputation as one of the greatest generals of all time (336 BC).

Roman legionaries, the finest foot soldiers of the ancient world, extend Rome's rule (241 BC–AD 107) from the shores of the Caspian Sea in the east to Spain's Atlantic coast in the west, and from Britain in the north to Egypt in the south—an empire served by almost 50,000 miles of military highways.

The Huns sweep into Europe from central Asia, precipitating a mass migration that will eventually destroy the Roman Empire in the west (370).

500–1500

The Frankish leader Charles Martel, having repelled the Moorish invasion of France (732), goes on to create a defense system centered on a professional class of mounted warriors.

Pope Urban II denounces the use of the crossbow in wars between Christians (1096). European knights embark on the First Crusade, following an appeal by the Pope to free Jerusalem from Muslim rule (1097).

English archers at the Battle of Crécy vanquish the armored cavalry of the French, thus heralding the demise of the feudal knight (1346).

French and Spanish forces fighting in Italy demonstrate the battle-winning potential of gunpowder weapons (1494-1559).

THE AMERICAS

500–1500

The Aztecs, armed with bows and arrows, slings, and swords with obsidian blades, subdue rival city-states to amass an empire in Central America (fifteenth century).

THE MIDDLE EAST AND AFRICA

10,000 BC–AD 500

Conflict among settled communities in Mesopotamia leads to the emergence of the first armies (c.10,000 BC).

The spear is supplemented by the bow and the sling (c.10,000 BC).

Jericho, probably the first fortified settlement, is founded in the Jordan Valley (c.8000 BC).

Bronze is used to make weapons and armor (c.3000 BC).

War chariots are introduced by the Sumerians (c.3000 BC).

Armed with iron weapons, the Assyrians become the greatest military power in the Middle East (c.900 BC).

The Phoenicians launch the first warships (c.700 BC).

500–1500

Inspired by the belief that death in battle will win them admission to paradise, Muslim armies erupt out of the Arabian Peninsula to found an empire stretching from the Punjab to the Pyrenees (c.700).

Arab armies besieging the Byzantine capital of Constantinople are driven back with a devastating weapon—the incendiary liquid known as Greek fire (717-718).

ASIA

10,000 BC–AD 500

Sun-tzu, a Chinese general, publishes *The Art of War*, the earliest-known treatise on the subject (c.500 BC).

500–1500

The Chinese produce the first gunpowder weapons (c.850).

Led by Genghis Khan, the Mongols sweep out of central Asia to defeat the armies of three continents and create the greatest empire the world has yet known (1211).

The Byzantine capital of Constantinople is battered into submission by the siege guns of the Ottoman Turks (1453).

TimeFrame 10,000 BC-AD 1990

500-1800	1800-1900	1900-1990
tch jurist and theologian Hugo Grotius publishes *On e Law of War and Peace*, setting out the fundamen- s of international law (1625).	Napoleon's defeat at the Battle of Waterloo (1815) ush- ers in almost one-half century of relative peace.	Antagonism between the European powers triggers the First World War, a conflict that will claim some 30 mil- lion casualties (1914-1918).
edish monarch Gustavus Adolphus uses the tech- que of volley firing to rout his Hapsburg opponents at e Battle of Breitenfeld during the Thirty Years' War 631).	*On War* by the German general Carl von Clausewitz is published, establishing guidelines for future generations of military strategists (1833).	The widespread bombing of cities during World War II (1939-1945) shatters the traditional distinction between combatants and civilians.
e Ottoman Turks lay siege to Vienna but are ham- red by the clumsiness of their artillery (1683).	Russian armored gunships destroy a Turkish frigate squadron at Sinope, sounding the death knell for fight- ing vessels made only of wood (1853).	Determined to achieve nuclear parity with the United States, the Soviet Union successfully detonates its first atomic weapon. The North Atlantic Treaty Organiza-
atchlock firearms are replaced by the more efficient ntlock musket (1690s).	The Crimean War (1853-1856) between Russia and the allied powers of France, Britain, and Turkey sees the first use of rifled artillery, torpedoes, and floating mines.	tion (NATO) brings together the United States, Canada, and ten nations of Western Europe in a defensive alli- ance (1949).
e French Revolution (1789) paves the way for Napo- on Bonaparte's campaigns of conquest.	At the Battle of Sadowa, Prussian troops armed with breechloading rifles defeat an Austrian army equipped with old-fashioned muzzleloaders (1866).	With the holding of free elections in Eastern Europe, the NATO powers and the Soviet Union proclaim the end of the Cold War (1990).

		Outraged at the sinking of its ships by German subma- rines, the United States declares war on Germany (1917).
		The dropping by the United States of atomic bombs on Hiroshima and Nagasaki forces the surrender of Japan and marks the beginning of the nuclear age (1945).
uipped with horses, firearms, and cannon, a small rce of Spaniards under the command of Hernán rtés conquers the Aztec empire of Mexico (1519- 21).		The United States test fires its first hydrogen bomb and builds its first nuclear-powered submarine (1952).
	The American Civil War (1861-1865) is the first major conflict to be dominated by the rifle—a weapon that proves deadly against frontal attacks.	The USSR pulls back from the threat of a nuclear con- frontation by accepting American demands that it should close down its missile bases in Cuba (1962).
nerican colonists, using a mixture of guerrilla and nventional tactics, win their war of independence ainst Britain (1775-1783).		The United States and Soviet Union begin strategic arms limitation talks (SALT), the first in a series of ne- gotiations aimed at controlling or reducing nuclear weapons (1969).

	European soldiers armed with rifles, machine guns, and field artillery carve out huge empires in Africa and in- ner Asia (1850-1900).	Iran and Iraq fight the longest conventional war since 1945: Both sides use long-range missiles, and more than one million front-line troops are killed in eight years of fighting (1980-1988).

		In a war between Russia and Japan, an Asian nation defeats a great European power for the first time (1904-1905).
Panipat, in a battle involving artillery, musketeers, valry, and war elephants, Bābur of Afghanistan de- ats the sultan of Delhi, thus laying the foundations of e Mogul empire (1526).		The Ottoman Empire enters World War I on the side of Germany; Japan goes to war as a British ally (1914).
		Japan uses aircraft carriers to launch an aerial attack on the U.S. Pacific naval base at Pearl Harbor (1941).
usketeers firing in continuous volleys destroy oncom- g Samurai cavalry at the battle of Nagashino in Japan 575).		China explodes its first atomic bomb (1964).
		South Vietnam surrenders to the Communist North af- ter U.S. troops withdraw, ending more than forty years of almost continuous fighting in the region (1975).
rean admiral Yi Sun-yin uses armorplated warships wreak havoc on the wooden hulls of an attacking panese fleet (1592).		After ten years of unsuccessful battling against Muslim tribesmen, Soviet troops hand over control to the Com- munist rulers of Afghanistan and return home (1989).

ACKNOWLEDGMENTS

The following material has been reprinted with the kind permission of the publishers: Page 17: "Like the oncoming of a storm I broke loose . . ." quoted in *The Origins of War,* by Arthur Ferrill, London: Thames and Hudson, 1986.

The editors also wish to thank the following individuals and institutions for their valuable assistance in the preparation of this volume:

England: Cambridge—David Lee, Imperial War Museum, Duxford Airfield. London—Lesley Coleman; Paul Dowswell; John Larkworthy, Wallace Collection; Deborah Pownall; Moira Thunder, Department of Prints and Drawings, Victoria and Albert Museum. Newcastle—J. M. Black.

BIBLIOGRAPHY

Adcock, Sir Frank E., *The Greek and Macedonian Art of War.* Berkeley: University of California Press, 1957.

Austin, M. M., ed., *The Hellenistic World from Alexander to the Roman Conquest: A Selection of Ancient Sources in Translation.* Cambridge: Cambridge University Press, 1981.

Bond, Brian, *War and Society in Europe 1870-1970.* London: Fontana Press, 1986.

Brent, Peter, *The Mongol Empire: Genghis Khan, His Triumph and His Legacy.* London: Weidenfeld and Nicolson, 1976.

Brereton, John M., *The Horse in War.* Newton Abbot, Devon: David & Charles, 1976.

Brogan, Patrick, *World Conflicts: Why and Where They are Happening.* London: Bloomsbury, 1989.

Caesar, Julius, *The Conquest of Gaul.* Transl. by S. A. Handford. London: Penguin Books, 1982.

Caven, Brian, *The Punic Wars.* London: Weidenfeld and Nicolson, 1980.

Cipolla, Carlo M., *Guns and Sails in the Early Phase of European Expansion 1400-1700.* London: Collins, 1965.

Cleator, P. E., *Weapons of War.* New York: Crowell, 1967.

Coblentz, Stanton A., *From Arrow to Atom Bomb: The Psychological History of War.* London: Peter Owen, 1986.

Connolly, Peter, *Greece and Rome at War.* London: Macdonald, 1981.

Contamine, Philippe, *War in the Middle Ages.* Transl. by Michael Jones. Oxford: Basil Blackwell, 1984.

Davis, R. H. C., *The Medieval Warhorse: Origin, Development and Redevelopment.* London: Thames and Hudson, 1989.

Duffy, Christopher:
Fire and Stone: The Science of Fortress Warfare 1660-1860. Newton Abbot, Devon: David & Charles, 1975.
The Military Experience in the Age of Reason. London: Routledge & Kegan Paul, 1987.
Siege Warfare, Vols. 1 and 2. London: Routledge & Kegan Paul, 1979, 1985.

Dupuy, R. Ernest, and Trevor N. Dupuy, eds., *The Encyclopedia of Military History: From 3500 BC to the Present.* London: Macdonald, 1970.

Dupuy, Trevor N., *The Evolution of Weapons and Warfare.* Fairfax, Virginia: Hero Books, 1984.

Edge, David, and John Miles Paddock, *Arms and Armour of the Medieval Knight.* London: Defoe, 1988.

Ferrill, Arthur:
The Fall of the Roman Empire: The Military Explanation. London: Thames and Hudson, 1986.
The Origins of War: From the Stone Age to Alexander the Great. London: Thames and Hudson, 1985.

Fox, Robin Lane, *Alexander the Great.* London: Penguin Books, 1986.

Fuller, Major General J. F. C., *The Decisive Battles of the Western World.* Vol. 1. London: Grafton Books, 1970.

Gabrieli, Francesco, ed., *Arab Historians of the Crusades.* Transl. by E. J. Costello. London: Routledge & Kegan Paul, 1969.

Gardner, Brian, *The Big Push: A Portrait of the Battle of the Somme.* London: Cassell, 1961.

Garlan, Yvon, *War in the Ancient World: A Social History.* Transl. by Janet Lloyd. London: Chatto & Windus, 1975.

Gies, Frances, *The Knight in History.* New York: Harper & Row, 1984.

Glover, Michael, *Warfare from Waterloo to Mons.* London: Cassell, 1980.

Hackett, General Sir John, *The Profession of Arms.* New York: Macmillan, 1983.

Hackett, General Sir John, ed., *Warfare in the Ancient World.* London: Sidgwick & Jackson, 1989.

Hale, John R.:
Renaissance War Studies. London: Hambledon Press, 1983.
War and Society in Renaissance Europe, 1450-1620. London: Fontana, 1985.

Headrick, Daniel R.:
Tentacles of Progress. New York: Oxford University Press, 1988.
The Tools of Empire: Technology and European Imperialism in the Nineteenth Century. New York: Oxford University Press, 1981.

Held, Robert, *The Age of Firearms: A Pictorial History.* London: Cassell, 1959.

Herodotus, *The Histories.* Transl. by Aubrey De Selincourt. London: Penguin Books, 1971.

Hibberd, Dominic, *The First World War.* Basingstoke: Macmillan, 1990.

Hinsley, F. H., *Power and the Pursuit of Peace.* Cambridge: Cambridge University Press, 1967.

Hitti, Philip K., *History of the Arabs.* London: Macmillan, 1970.

Hogg, Ian V., *Fortress: A History of Military Defence.* London: Macdonald and Jane's, 1975.

Holmes, Richard, *Firing Line.* London: Penguin Books, 1987.

Holt, P. M., *The Age of the Crusades: The Near East from the Eleventh Century to 1517.* New York: Longman, 1986.

Hopkins, Andrea, *Knights.* London: Collins & Brown, 1990.

Howard, Michael:
War and the Liberal Conscience. New Brunswick, New Jersey: Rutgers University Press, 1978.
War in European History. Oxford: Oxford University Press, 1976.

Hughes, Basil P., *Firepower: Weapons Effectiveness on the Battlefield.* London: Arms & Armour Press, 1974.

Humble, Richard, *Warfare in the Ancient World.* London: Cassell, 1980.

Johnson, James Turner, *The Quest for Peace.* Princeton: Princeton University Press, 1987.

Jones, Archer, *The Art of War in the Western World.* Urbana-Champaign, Illinois: University of Illinois Press, 1987.

Josephus, Flavius, *The Jewish War.* Transl. by G. A. Williamson. London: Penguin Books, 1981.

Keegan, John, and Richard Holmes, *Soldiers: A History of Men in Battle.* London: Hamish Hamilton, 1985.

Liddle, Peter H.:
The Soldier's War 1914-18. London: Blandford Press, 1988.
Voices of War: Front Line and Home Front. London: Leo Cooper, 1988.

Lloyd, Alan, *Destroy Carthage! The Death Throes of an Ancient Culture.* London: Souvenir Press, 1977.

Luttwak, Edward N., *The Grand Strategy of the Roman Empire: From the First Century AD to the Third.* Baltimore: Johns Hopkins University Press, 1976.

Maalouf, Amin, *The Crusades through Arab Eyes.* Transl. by Jon Rothschild. London: Al Saqi Books, 1984.

McNeill, William H., *The Pursuit of Power: Technology, Armed Force, and Society Since AD 1000.* Chicago: University of Chicago Press, 1982.

Mallet, Michael E., *Mercenaries and Their Masters: Warfare in Renaissance Italy.* London: Bodley Head, 1974.

Martin, Colin, and Geoffrey Parker, *The Spanish Armada.* New York: Norton, 1988.

Montgomery of Alamein, Field Marshal Viscount, *A History of Warfare.* London: Collins, 1968.

Moon, Sir Penderel, *The British Conquest and Dominion of India.* London: Duckworth, 1989.

Morgan, David, *The Mongols.* Oxford: Basil Blackwell, 1986.

Nansen, Fridtjof, *Eskimo Life.* London: Longmans, Green & Co., 1893.

Needham, Joseph, *Science and Civilisation in China.* Vol. 5, Part 7. Cambridge: Cambridge University Press, 1986.

Newark, Peter, *Sabre & Lance: An Illustrated History of Cavalry.* Poole, Dorset: Blandford Press, 1987.

Newark, Timothy, *Medieval Warfare: An Illustrated Introduction.* London: Jupiter Press, 1988.

Norman, A. V. B., and Don Pottinger, *A History of War and Weapons, 449 to 1660.* New York: Crowell, 1967.

O'Connell, Robert L., *Of Arms and Men: A History of War, Weapons, and Aggression.* New York: Oxford University Press, 1989.

Oman, Sir Charles, *A History of the Art of War in the Middle Ages.* London: Methuen, 1924.

Paret, Peter, ed., *Makers of Modern Strategy: From Machiavelli to the Nuclear Age.* Oxford: Clarendon Press, 1990.

Parker, Geoffrey, *The Military Revolution: Military Innovation and the Rise of the West, 1500-1800.* Cambridge: Cambridge University Press, 1988.

Pepper, Simon, and Nicholas Adams, *Firearms & Fortifications: Military Architecture and Siege Warfare in Sixteenth-Century Siena.* Chicago: University of Chicago Press, 1986.

Perrin, Noel, *Giving Up the Gun: Japan's Reversion to the Sword 1543-1879.* London: Routledge, 1977.

Pfeiffer, John E., *The Emergence of Humankind.* New York: Harper & Row, 1985.

Pope, Dudley, *Guns.* London: Weidenfeld & Nicolson, 1965.

Reid, William, *Weapons through the Ages.* London: Peerage Books, 1984.

Rhodes, Richard, *The Making of the Atomic Bomb.* London: Penguin Books, 1988.

Robinson, Basil W., *The Arts of the Japanese Sword.* London: Faber and Faber, 1970.

Rothenberg, Gunther E., *The Art of Warfare in the Age of Napoleon.* London: B. T. Batsford, 1977.

Saggs, H. W. F., *The Might That Was Assyria.* London: Sidgwick & Jackson, 1984.

Smail, R. C., *Crusading Warfare (1097-1193).* Cambridge: Cambridge University Press, 1956.

Snodgrass, A. M., *Arms and Armour of the Greeks.* London: Thames and Hudson, 1967.

Strachan, Hew, *European Armies and the Conduct of War.* London: George Allen & Unwin, 1983.

Sun-tzu, *The Art of War.* Transl. by Thomas Cleary. Boston: Shambhala, 1988.

Tacitus, *The Agricola and the Germania.* Transl. by H. Mattingly. London: Penguin Books, 1970.

Taylor, Philip M., *Munitions of the Mind: War Propaganda from the Ancient World to the Nuclear Age.* London: Patrick Stephens, 1990.

Turnbull, Stephen, *Samurai Warriors.* London: Blandford Press, 1987.

Van Creveld, Martin:
Supplying War: Logistics from Wallenstein to Patton. Cambridge: Cambridge University Press, 1977.
Technology and War: From 2000 BC to the Present. London: Macmillan, 1989.

Vernant, Jean-Pierre, *Myth and Society in Ancient Greece.* Transl. by Janet Lloyd. Brighton, East Sussex: Harvester, 1980.

Warner, Philip, *Firepower: From Slings to Star Wars.* London: Grafton Books, 1989.

Warry, John, *Warfare in the Classical World.* London: Salamander, 1980.

White, Lynn, *Mediaeval Technology and Social Change.* New York: Oxford University Press, 1962.

Winter, J. M., *The Experience of World War I.* London: Macmillan, 1988.

Yadin, Yigael, *The Art of Warfare in Biblical Lands.* London: Weidenfeld and Nicolson, 1963.

PICTURE CREDITS

The sources for the illustrations that appear in this book are listed below. Credits from left to right are separated by semicolons; from top to bottom they are separated by dashes.

Cover: Detail from painting *The Battle of the Pyramids, 21 July 1798* by Léjeune, Réunion des Musées Nationaux, Paris. **2-3:** Bulloz, Paris. **8:** Trustees of the British Museum, London. **10:** Scala, Florence / Cortile delle Corazze, Vatican, Rome—art by Jonothan Potter. **13:** Trustees of the British Museum, London. **14:** Lauros-Giraudon, Paris. **16:** Ingrid Geske / SMPK Antikenmuseum, Berlin. **18:** Scala, Florence / Museo di Villa Giulia, Rome. **20-21:** Trustees of the British Museum, London. **24:** Michael Holford, Loughton, Essex / Collection British Museum, London—Werner Forman Archive, London / The University Museum, Oslo. **25:** By permission of the India Office Library (British Library), London, Ethe 2992 f.121v. **28, 29:** Michael Holford, Loughton, Essex / Collection British Museum, London (2). **30, 31:** Aerofilms, Borehamwood, Hertfordshire—by permission of the British Library, London, Add. 23920/43; Ekdotike Athenon S.A., Athens. **32:** National Museums of Scotland, Edinburgh—map by Alan Hollingbery. **35:** Trustees of the British Museum, London. **36:** Robert Harding Picture Library, London. **37:** E. T. Archive, London. **38:** By permission of the British Library, London, Add. 23920 fol. 50. **39:** The Hulton Picture Company, London. **40:** By permission of the British Library, London, MS. Roy 6EX1 f.24. **42-43:** The Pierpoint Morgan Library, New York, M.638 f.23v. **44:** Richard Pearce / Wiltshire Archaeological and Natural History Society, Devizes, Wiltshire. **45:** The Board of Trustees of the Royal Armouries, London. **47:** By permission of the British Library, London, 779K8 p. 29. **48-49:** Michael Holford, Loughton, Essex (4). **50:** Werner Forman Archive, London / Kita-In, Saitama, Japan. **51:** Werner Forman Archive, London /

Victoria and Albert Museum, London; Werner Forman Archive, London / Bethnal Green Museum, London. **53:** By permission of the British Library, London, 16GV1 404v. **54:** Map by Alan Hollingbery—Robin Constable / The Hutchison Library, London. **56:** Edinburgh University Library, Edinburgh. **60, 61:** Hilbinger / Stadtbibliothek Nürnberg, Nuremberg, Amb. 317.2o f.147v; reproduced by permission of the Trustees, The Wallace Collection, London; art by Jonothan Potter (2). **62:** By permission of the British Library, London. **64-65:** The Fotomas Index, London. **66:** Réunion des Musées Nationaux, Paris, courtesy Musée Guimet. **69:** By permission of the British Library, London, 718.K.28(3) f.L1v. **70-72:** Museum of the History of Art, Collection Sculpture and Crafts, Vienna. **73:** By permission of the British Library, London, 1B 30748 X.Sy.Dvi—Guildhall Library, London. **77:** By permission of the British Library, London, C27921—Weidenfeld and Nicolson Ltd., London. **78:** Courtesy of the Board and Trustees of the Victoria and Albert Museum, London. **80, 81:** By permission of the British Library, London (2), Cott.Aug. li 21 and 62.d.3. p. 146. **83:** Ullstein Bilderdienst, Berlin. **84:** By permission of the British Library, London, c133d8. **86, 87:** Map by Alan Hollingbery; by permission of the India Office Library (British Library), London, I.O. Album 58 p. 5346 *(inset)*. **88, 89:** The Mansell Collection, London; Peter A. Clayton, Hemel Hempstead, Hertfordshire. **90, 91:** Robert Hunt Library, London; by permission of the British Library, London *(inset)*. **92, 93:** Peter Newark's Military Pictures, Bath; C. M. Dixon, Canterbury, Kent—Robert Hunt Library, London. **94, 95:** Robert Hunt Library, London; The Hulton Picture Company, London. **96:** Trustees of the Imperial War Museum, London. **98:** Trustees of the Imperial War Museum, London. **100-101:** *The Illustrated London News* Picture Library, London. **104-105:** *The Illustrated London News* Picture Library, London. **106:** Trustees of the Imperial War Museum, London (2). **108, 109:** Trustees of the

Imperial War Museum, London (2). **112, 113:** Trustees of the Imperial War Museum, London; The Hulton Picture Company, London. **114:** Trustees of the Imperial War Museum, London. **117:** Trustees of the Imperial War Museum, London (2). **118:** Trustees of the Imperial War Museum, London; Robert Hunt Library, London. **121:** Trustees of the Imperial War Museum, London. **123:** The Hulton Picture Company, London (2). **125:** Adrian C. Smith, Taunton, Somerset. **127:** Reproduced by kind permission of His Grace the Duke of Marlborough. Photograph by Jeremy Whittaker. **128, 129:** By permission of the British Library, London, 718.K.28; Trustees of the Imperial War Museum, London. **130, 131:** Michael Holford, Loughton, Essex / Collection British Museum, London—The Fotomas Index, London. **132, 133:** Wellcome Institute Library, London; Ullstein Bilderdienst, Berlin—Trustees of the Imperial War Museum, London. **134, 135:** By permission of the British Library, London, 718.K.28 (3) f.LXV; UPI / Bettman, New York. **136:** The Associated Press, London. **138-139:** U.S. Air Force. **140, 141:** Mary Evans Picture Library, London—Eastfoto, New York; Trustees of the Imperial War Museum, London; Setboun / Rex Features Limited, London. **144:** Art by Jonothan Potter. **145:** Robert Hunt Library, London; Trustees of the Imperial War Museum, London. **146:** Art by Jonothan Potter; Trustees of the Imperial War Museum, London. **147:** Ullstein Bilderdienst, Berlin. **148, 149:** Art by Jonothan Potter; Trustees of the Imperial War Museum, London (2). **150, 151:** Art by Jonothan Potter; Trustees of the Imperial War Museum, London (2). **152:** Map by Alan Hollingbery. **153:** Ken Sherman, Friar's Hill, West Virginia. **154:** The Hulton Picture Company, London; Popperfoto, London. **155:** The Tate Gallery, London. **156-157:** Topham, Edenbridge, Kent. **158:** Robert Hunt Library, London. **160-161:** Lena Kara / Rex Features Limited, London. **164-165:** Steve McCurry / Magnum, London.

INDEX